"A twin pack of pleasure: First we get Brooks Headley's terrific writing and then his great recipes. All the SB favorites are here, all the off-beat combinations—I think of them as Brooksisms— and all the good instructions we need to make this **DEEPLY SATISFYING** food at home. It's such an exciting book!"

—DORIE GREENSPAN,
author of *Dorie's Cookies* and *Everyday Dorie*

"In an alternate universe Superiority Burger is bigger than McDonald's, all the Ramones, Slits, and Prince are **STILL ALIVE**, and everyone is **HAPPY**. Until then, we have this cookbook."

—KERRY DIAMOND, editor of *CHERRY BOMBE MAGAZINE*

"No idle boasting here—this vegetarian hotspot lives up to the name, and Superiority is my first stop upon arrival in NYC. This **UNIQUE COOKBOOK** reveals the **MAGICAL SECRETS** of a one-of-a-kind menu that puts the competition to shame."

—NEIL HAMBURGER, America's $1 Funnyman

"Rarely is a pastry chef able to make the transition from sweets to savory as seamlessly as Brooks Headley. Once again, Brooks' creativity is on display in *Superiority Burger Cookbook*. The recipes are mouthwatering and I can't wait to get my hands on it."

—CLAUDIA FLEMING, chef and author of *The Last Course*

"Eruptions of molten fruit magma, pump cheese, and rutabagas. As vibrant a book as New York City itself."

—MEREDITH ERICKSON,
author of *The Art of Living According to Joe Beef* and *Claridge's Cookbook*

SUPE RIORITY BU RGER

ALSO BY BROOKS HEADLEY

Brooks Headley's Fancy Desserts:
The Recipes of Del Posto's James Beard Award–Winning Pastry Chef

Superiority Burger Cookbook

The Vegetarian Hamburger Is Now Delicious

Brooks Headley

with Julia Goldberg, Gabe Rosner,
Matthew Silverstein, and Matt Sweeney

Photographs by
Sunny Shokrae

W. W. Norton & Company
Independent Publishers Since 1923
New York / London

For information about permission to reproduce
selections from this book, write to
Permissions, W. W. Norton & Company, Inc.,
500 Fifth Avenue, New York, NY 10110

For information about special discounts for bulk
purchases, please contact W. W. Norton
Special Sales at specialsales@wwnorton.com or
800-233-4830

Manufacturing by Versa Press
Book design by Walter Green

ISBN 978-0-393-25398-6

W. W. Norton & Company, Inc.
500 Fifth Avenue, New York, N.Y. 10110
www.wwnorton.com

W. W. Norton & Company Ltd.
15 Carlisle Street, London W1D 3BS

2 3 4 5 6 7 8 9 0

CONTENTS

Superiority Burger Cookbook

INTRODUCTION

EVERYTHING IS VEGETARIAN, A LOT IS
ACCIDENTALLY VEGAN, JUST ASK

Superiority Burger opened at 430 East 9th Street in the East Village of Manhattan on June 25, 2015. Our goal was (and is) to provide vegetarian food of a modest, non-fancy nature, and sell it for as cheaply as possible while still using the best ingredients we can find. We have five swing desks that can accommodate a total of between six and nine humans, depending on how cozy folks want to get. A lot of people get food to take away. Sometimes, weather-permitting, our customers will eat on the sidewalk, sitting on various benches and planters nearby. Tompkins Square Park is 300 feet away; there are park benches there too. All of our food is served in paper boats and is meant to be eaten with biodegradable plastic utensils.

Our space is diminutive—275 square feet, including the dining area. Our firepower is limited; we have a steel griddle to cook burgers, four induction burners, and a small inherited convection oven that accepts only half sheet pans. Anything we can make here you can also do at home.

The name of our restaurant is Superiority Burger, but that's a bit of a red herring. Sure, the majority of our business is selling vegetarian hamburgers, but you can cobble together a very nice meal here and avoid the burger altogether. In addition to our sandwiches, sides, and desserts, we offer a single drink, a house-made Arnold Palmer served over pellet ice. We don't sell alcohol. We don't sell bottled water. We think it's strange and a con for any restaurant to *sell* non-fizzy water. There is always a plastic jug of lemon juice–spiked NYC tap water at the ready in the dining room. We refill it as fast as our customers drink it, and it is always cold and refreshing. In terms of beverage pairings for any of the recipes in this book, chilled lemon water is the way to go.

Sometimes people refer to us as a fast-food joint. This is only moderately correct. Yes, we try to push out orders as quickly as possible, but sometimes things take a little longer than expected. We are not trying to compete with fast-food establishments. But we do take a hospitality and service approach not unlike fancy, fine-dining restaurants, where a few of us honed our chops and licks.

This cookbook is a document of just about everything we have sold on our main menu and specials board. There are probably some new things since this book went to print; we tend to work fast and in spurts.

Our specials change around a lot when we are feeling particularly inspired and unhinged, and sometimes they hover on a few very good seasonal things that we run until nature stops providing the raw material.

We have never served French fries, fresh-cut or frozen. We do not have a deep fryer.

We cook mostly from a vegan perspective, but do use some dairy sparingly (nondairy options are given for all recipes except for the gelatos—we have yet to crack a vegan gelato code that we feel confident to share publicly, but the coconut sorbet is dairy-free and about as creamy and rich as you could ever want).

We have a photo of actual meat on the wall, in the form of a vintage 1992 White Castle ad (we love White Castle, no joking around). But we are very serious about the vegetarian cooking that goes on here.

THANK YOU.

A FEW NOTES ON THESE RECIPES

SALT is kosher and is a given for every recipe (yes, even the sorbets!), even when not mentioned in the ingredients lists. Freshly ground pepper is also standard in almost every savory recipe. Add as much or as little as you prefer. Salt is listed by measurement only in the more exact recipes, like pickled vegetables, spice blends, and cakes. Otherwise, assume you will be adding salt and pepper to the seasoning to your liking. We use lots. But never too much. Sea salt is A-OK too, just be careful as it can be finer grained, therefore more potent.

SUGAR is unbleached organic cane sugar unless specified otherwise.

FLOUR is all-purpose.

WATER. Do not underestimate its power. It can thin out an overreduced soup, and it can soften stuff up in a frying pan. Use it wisely and safely.

SPICES are purchased from a reliable purveyor and ground the day of or day before doing the recipe. The spices will always taste better, fresher, and more intense. An inexpensive coffee grinder will work nicely for this.

GRAPESEED OIL is fine for cooking and frying. Sometimes we use a mid-range **EXTRA VIRGIN OLIVE OIL** for cooking as well. Really nice (read: expensive) olive oils are reserved for final garnishing and seasoning right before serving, because olive oil is the best sauce.

We use Hodo Soy–brand **TOFU AND YUBA**. It's expensive, but it has no equal.

For all **BROWN RICE** applications we use Koda Farms organic brown rice. It deeply transcends regular brown rice.

This book is 95 percent vegan, the exception being a scant use of milk, milk powder, cream (gelato recipes), and labne (in a few different recipes). A high-quality soy, cashew, or coconut vegan yogurt can be substituted for any of the dairy components. We do not use eggs or butter.

We use Gulden's brown mustard, B&G hot cherry peppers, Frank's RedHot, Matouk's Calypso, Delouis Dijon, Bragg Liquid Aminos, and Heinz organic ketchup. Some things are just better *not* homemade. We feel strongly about this. But we would never use commercial mayonnaise (vegan or real). We use only the chickpea recipe on page 211. This may seem contradictory. We are fine with that.

We have a firm commitment to farmers' market fruits, herbs, and vegetables. But if you can't find what you need there due to seasonal availability, then supermarket produce is fine. It will just need a little extra help, but that's what cooking is, right?

Whenever dried **PASTA** is mentioned, go for the blue box of De Cecco. It's widely available and texturally fantastic when cooked to al dente.

Our **POLENTA** is from Anson Mills in South Carolina. They ship all over. Support these guys and use their stuff. It's perishable so keep it refrigerated. It's of a completely different caliber from any other polenta you can grab at the supermarket or even that fancy-food shop, the one with the inflated pricing.

We have tried to keep the recipes easy to follow and all on one page. However, a few require using additional recipes found in the back pantry section (see page 203). You will get to know these pantry recipes very well.

All of the **MEASUREMENTS** are in cups and tablespoons; that's how we cook at the restaurant. Our gelato formula is in metric, though. So you will need a scale, but only for that recipe. An Escali Primo scale is about forty bucks, industry standard, and will never let you down. You will also need a working candy thermometer for the gelato recipe; we love our Thermapen.

There isn't a standard recipe portion size. If it's a little annoying, we apologize. Some things work well for four portions, and some things just make more sense for six or eight. Either way, all this stuff makes for fantastic leftovers, so look forward to that at 2 a.m., or for breakfast the next day.

Sandwiches

SUPERIORITY BURGER

MAKES 8 TO 10 PATTIES

1 cup red quinoa

1 medium yellow
onion, chopped

2 teaspoons ground toasted
fennel seeds

1 teaspoon chile powder

1 cup cooked chickpeas,
rinsed and drained

1 teaspoon white wine vinegar

1 cup small-diced carrots

½ cup coarse bread crumbs

¾ cup walnuts, toasted
and crushed

Juice of 1 lemon

1 tablespoon chopped fresh
flat-leaf parsley

1 tablespoon hot chile sauce

2 tablespoons nonmodified
potato starch

Grapeseed oil for searing
the patties

Toasted buns/shredded
lettuce/roasted tomatoes/2
pickle slices/Muenster
cheese (if you like)/sauces
(honey mustard, Special
Sauce) of your choice
for serving

This is not fake meat, nor is it vying to be. The un-likeness to the real thing is canny. Think of these as vegetable and grain croquettes that get put on buns. These are our namesake, they are absolutely recognizable as food, and are meant to be a Luddite response to the modern gaggle of vegetable patties that bleed and squirt and ape.

Preheat the oven to 425°F.

Cook the quinoa in 1½ cups salted water until fluffy, about 45 minutes. Cool and reserve. In a separate pan, sauté the onion until translucent and browned, and season with salt, pepper, the fennel, and chile powder. Add the chickpeas and keep on the heat for 5 to10 minutes, stirring constantly. Deglaze the hot pan with the white wine vinegar and scrape everything stuck to the bottom of the pan back into the mix. Using a potato masher, roughly smash the onion-chickpea mixture. Mix the chickpea mash by hand with the cooled quinoa.

Roast the carrots in the oven until dark around the edges and soft, about 25 minutes. Add to the chickpea-quinoa mixture. Add the bread crumbs, walnuts, lemon, parsley, and chile sauce, and season again with salt and pepper, until it tastes sharp. Mix the potato starch with 1 tablespoon water to create a cloudy, thick slurry. Fold the slurry into the burger mix as the binding agent. Form the mixture into 8 to 10 patties and sear in grapeseed oil in a hot sauté pan or cast-iron skillet until fully browned, about 3 minutes on each side. To serve, place each patty on a toasted bun with shredded iceberg lettuce, Roasted Red Tomatoes (page 71), 2 pickle slices, Muenster cheese (if you like), and sauces such as honey mustard or Special Sauce (page 212).

SLOPPY DAVE

SERVES 8

2 large Spanish onions

3 celery stalks

1 green bell pepper

3 scallions

3 pickled cherry peppers,
   stems removed

4 tablespoons extra
   virgin olive oil

2 tablespoons tomato paste

3 tablespoons chile powder

1½ tablespoons ground cumin

1 tablespoon Korean
   chile flakes

¼ cup cider vinegar

Two 15-ounce cans
   crushed tomatoes

¼ cup ketchup

2 tablespoons dark brown sugar

2 tablespoons Dijon mustard

3 tablespoons Bragg
   Liquid Aminos

1½ teaspoons freshly ground
   black pepper

2 pounds extra firm
   tofu, drained

Toasted sesame seed buns

Frizzled Onions
   (recipe follows)

We originally listed this on our menu as a sloppy joe, until we realized that most of these were being sold to our friend and neighbor Dave. Dave doesn't get "sloppy" anymore, and insisted we rename the sandwich in his teetotaling honor. He comes a few times a week with his lady, Uli, and their hound. Squishy. They almost always eat outside.

Roughly chop all the vegetables, including the cherry peppers, and process in batches in a food processor until finely chopped. Heat 3 tablespoons of the olive oil over medium heat in a big pot and add the processed vegetables. Salt. Cook until the veg is totally soft and takes on a little color, about 20 minutes. Add the tomato paste and spices and cook for another 10 minutes, stirring frequently. It is okay if it sticks to the bottom of the pot. Add the cider vinegar and scrape the bottom of the pot to get off all browned bits of vegetables and tomato paste.

Add the tomatoes, ketchup, brown sugar, mustard, 1 tablespoon of the amino acids, and the black pepper and bring to a boil. Reduce the heat and simmer for as long as you can—30 minutes will do. While the sauce is simmering, crumble the tofu. In a large skillet over medium heat, add the remaining 1 tablespoon oil and the tofu and brown. Once the tofu is mostly brown, pour in the remaining 2 tablespoons amino acids and let cook a bit longer, until the tofu absorbs all of the sauce and begins to caramelize. Remove from the heat and set aside.

Roughly grind the tofu in the food processor. Add the tofu to the pot of sauce and continue to cook. Season with salt and black pepper. Serve on a toasted sesame seed bun. Top with frizzled onions.

FRIZZLED ONIONS

FOR 8 SLOPPY DAVES

2 Spanish onions

1 cup Wondra flour or
  rice flour

1 cup all-purpose flour

8 cups grapeseed oil for frying

Peel and cut the onions in half. Use a mandoline to cut paper thin. Mix the Wondra and all-purpose flours and season with salt and pepper. Heat the grapeseed oil in a heavy deep pot to about 350°F. Put the onions into the seasoned flour, toss to coat, shake off the excess flour, and carefully drop into the hot oil. Do not add too many at once—the oil will overflow and ruin everything. Using a slotted spoon, agitate and stir the onions until they are golden brown. Drain on paper towels and season with more salt. Repeat the frying process.

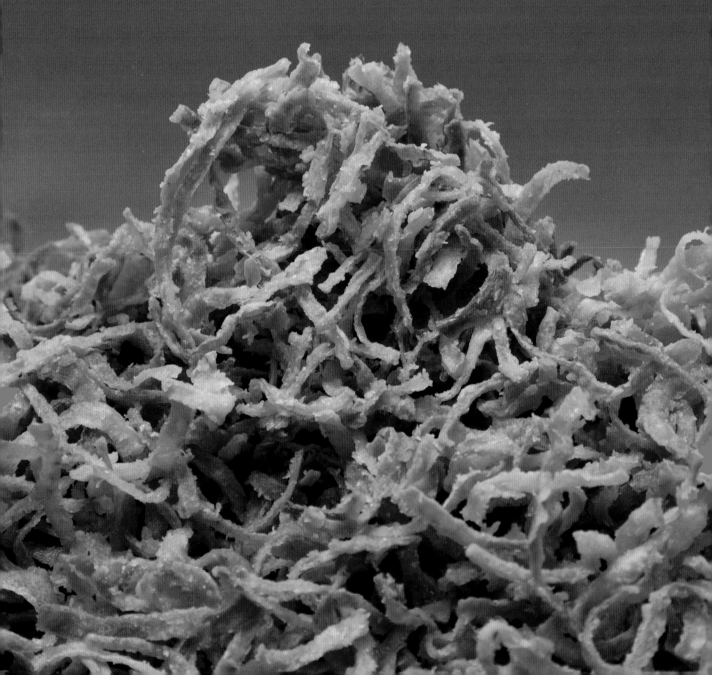

HIPPY WRAP

When we first opened, we tried to sell this and no one bought it. Humans have a very averse reaction to the word "hippy." We changed the name to Superiority Wrap and then people started purchasing it. It's meant to make fun of wraps, of vegetarian food in general, and quite possibly ourselves. All the health food tropes are here: carrots, sunflower seeds, tofu, brown rice, and cabbage, although the recipe is not technically "healthy." Our buddy Caroline who runs the unflappable restaurant Saltie in Brooklyn had one once and laughed as she ate it, obviously getting the joke.

HIPPY MIX

SERVES 4

1 knob celery root

2 tablespoons extra virgin
olive oil

2 tablespoons chile powder

1 tablespoon sweet paprika

½ teaspoon ground ginger

½ teaspoon ground coriander

¼ teaspoon ground cardamom

½ head green cabbage

1 cup golden balsamic vinegar

2 tablespoons Bragg
Liquid Aminos

1 tablespoon Dijon mustard

1 tablespoon maple syrup

½ block (1 pound) extra
firm tofu

2 tablespoons grapeseed oil

Preheat the oven to 400°F.

Peel and cut the celery root into small cubes. Toss with the olive oil, seasonings, and salt. Spread out the dressed cubes on a baking sheet—do not crowd them too much. Cook until slightly browned and tender, about 25 minutes. Set aside.

Turn off the oven and turn on the broiler. Cut the cabbage into ¼-inch ribbons. Spread into a single layer on a baking sheet. This does not require oil. Broil until the cabbage just starts to char, about 5 minutes. Set aside.

Whisk together the golden balsamic vinegar, amino acids, mustard, and maple syrup. Add a good pinch of salt and pepper. Drain the tofu and press out as much liquid as possible. Crumble the tofu into bite-size chunks with your hands. Heat the grapeseed oil in a large skillet over medium-high heat until shimmering. Add the tofu chunks and cook until they begin to take on color and crisp up, about 5 minutes. When all the pieces are well browned, reduce the heat to medium. Add the vinegar mixture to the pan and stir thoroughly until the tofu is coated with the sauce and it begins to evaporate, reduce, and caramelize. Remove the pan from the heat and pour the tofu into a large bowl. Add the celery root and cabbage to the bowl and mix to combine. Check for seasoning, adding salt and pepper as needed.

continues

SOOM SAUCE

MAKES ABOUT 1 CUP

¾ cup smooth tahini (we use
   Soom brand exclusively)

¼ to ½ cup water

2 tablespoons hot chile sauce

1 tablespoon maple syrup

1 tablespoon pickle juice

(we use leftover B&G cherry
   pepper juice)

In a large bowl, whisk together the tahini and enough water to start to thin out the tahini, about ¼ cup. The mixture should have the consistency of natural peanut butter. Whisk in the chile sauce, maple syrup, and pickle juice. Adjust the seasoning to taste with more of these things. Season with salt.

PICKLED CARROTS

MAKES 2 CUPS

1 pound carrots, sliced
   into matchsticks with a
   mandoline or by hand

1 tablespoon cane sugar

¼ cup extra virgin olive oil

Zest and juice of 1 lemon

¼ cup chopped fresh cilantro

1 Fresno chile, seeded and
   finely chopped

1 teaspoon ground cumin

½ teaspoon ground cinnamon

1 teaspoon New Mexican
   chile powder

2 cups white wine vinegar

Toss the carrots with the sugar and a large pinch of salt in a large bowl. Let stand for about 15 minutes, until the carrots start to release their juices. Add everything else—except the white wine vinegar—to the bowl and combine thoroughly. Transfer the carrots and any juice left in the bowl to a storage container with a lid, like a jar or quart container. Press the carrots down just a little bit. Add enough white wine vinegar to just cover the carrots. Lid and refrigerate until ready to use. These will keep for a few weeks in the refrigerator.

SUNFLOWER CRUNCH

MAKES 2 CUPS

2 cups raw shelled
   sunflower seeds

¼ cup simple syrup

¾ cup raw sugar

Preheat the oven to 325°F. Line a baking sheet with parchment paper.

Toss the sunflower seeds in the simple syrup in a medium bowl so they are thoroughly coated. Sprinkle in the sugar and a big pinch of salt and taste for seasoning—the mixture should be a well-balanced sweet and salty. Spread the seeds into a thin layer on the baking sheet. Bake for 15 minutes and check on them. Continue to bake, checking every 5 minutes or so, until they are a medium golden brown. Let cool, transfer to a plastic bag, and crush up with a rolling pin. Pack into an airtight container for up to 1 week until ready to use.

"SUPERIORITY" WRAP/BOAT ASSEMBLY

SERVES 4

Four 12-inch whole wheat
tortillas (if making wraps)

2 cups warm cooked brown rice
(page 211)

1 batch warm Hippy Mix
(page 26)

1 cup Soom Sauce (page 28)

2 cups Pickled Carrots (page 28)

2 celery stalks, cut into
small dice

1 cup Sunflower Crunch
(page 28)

If making the wrap, heat the tortillas, one at a time, in a large dry skillet until they are warm and just a little toasty on one side. Construct in this order: rice, hippy mix, soom sauce, carrots, celery, and sunflower crunch. Roll up like a burrito, making sure to fold in both sides and roll tightly. Wrap tightly again in a piece of aluminum foil. Cut in half or serve whole. If making the boat, follow the same order of construction, just in a bowl.

TOFU-FRIED TOFU

SERVES 4

1 pound extra firm tofu

1 teaspoon Korean chile flakes

1 tablespoon hot chile
  sauce (we use Matouk's
  Calypso sauce)

1 tablespoon Dijon mustard

1½ cups pickle juice

Grapeseed oil

½ cup Dijon mustard

4 cups all-purpose flour

1 teaspoon baking powder

2 teaspoons smoked paprika

½ teaspoon onion powder

½ teaspoon garlic powder

½ teaspoon cayenne pepper

1 teaspoon freshly ground
  black pepper

1½ teaspoons kosher salt

Buns/mayo/shredded
  cabbage/dill pickles
  for serving

Monday nights are often our slowest of the week. So we started offering this sandwich as a way to, in the words of Christina, one of our counter people, "lure some asses into the seats." Aesthetically, it is very similar to a fast-food fried chicken sandwich, minus the corporate and psychological guilt commonly associated with consuming commodity boneless, skinless chicken on a bun.

Cut the tofu into ½-inch rectangles. Arrange on a baking sheet lined with paper towels or a clean kitchen towel and cover with more towels. Apply pressure to remove some of the moisture. Mix together the chile flakes, hot sauce, the 1 tablespoon mustard, and the pickle juice in a large bowl. Heat a little bit of grapeseed oil in a large nonstick or cast-iron skillet until shimmering. Sear the tofu on both sides to get a golden brown crust. Immediately drop the hot tofu into the pickle juice mixture. Let the tofu sit in this liquid in the refrigerator for a few hours or even overnight.

Mix the ½ cup mustard with a little bit of water to make it the consistency of heavy cream. Set aside. Whisk together the flour, baking powder, and all the spices in a large shallow bowl. Heat 2 inches of grapeseed oil over medium heat in a deep, sturdy pot. Remove the tofu from the brine and pat dry. Dip the tofu in the watered-down mustard, then the flour, then the mustard again, and the flour. When the oil temperature reaches 350°F, carefully drop the battered tofu into the hot oil and fry, flipping as needed, until golden brown. Set the fried tofu on a wire rack on a baking sheet and immediately sprinkle with a little salt. Repeat until all the tofu is fried off. To serve, toast the buns and spread generously with mayo (we add a little Calypso sauce to make ours spicy). Top with thinly shredded cabbage and dill pickles. Eat immediately.

HAMMERED MUSHROOM SANDWICH

SERVES 1

Iceberg lettuce leaves

2 slices sourdough bread

Extra virgin olive oil

½ to ¾ cup Hammered
   Mushrooms (page 207)

2 tablespoons Chickpea Mayo
   (page 211)

1 tomato, the best you can
   find, sliced ¼ inch thick
   and aggressively salted
   and peppered

There's no point in messing around with this one unless there are peak August tomatoes at the greenmarket. This is about as simple as it gets. And that whole spiel where a puffed-up chef's marketing/PR assistant/propaganda spewer says, "We will just let the ingredients speak for themselves?" That baloney? That most certainly applies here (for once). Iceberg is here simply for water and cellulose, not to make anyone upset.

Trim the lettuce leaves to fit the bread. Heat a heavy skillet over medium heat, add a little olive oil, and toast the bread on one side until golden brown and crisp. Take the bread out of the pan and set aside for a minute. Add the mushrooms to the hot pan and cook for a minute, until they are warmed through. Spread the untoasted sides of the bread with the mayo. Top with the tomato slices, lettuce, and mushrooms. Eats well warm or at room temperature.

YUBA PHILADELPHIA/ NEW CREATION

Oakland, CA's Hodo Soy yuba is a very magical thing. It is highly perishable, neutral in flavor, takes on marinades stunningly, and is very fresh. Yuba is the skin that forms on top of simmering soy milk. It is hand harvested and is texturally right on. Our pal and neighbor Lagusta, who runs a confectionery shop a few doors down on East 9th Street, refers to yuba as "having the satisfying texture of meat while being wholly nonprocessed." She's right—it's just soybeans and water. Previous to discovering the Hodo brand, our yuba experiences were relegated to the dried packaged stuff that frequently tastes off and like chemicals.

YUBA PHILADELPHIA

MAKES 4 SANDWICHES

2 tablespoons grapeseed oil

2 medium red onions, thinly sliced

2 green bell peppers, thinly sliced

2 cups Marinated Yuba Strips (see page 210)

4 small potato rolls, regular or vegan

2 cups hot Pump Cheese (page 204)

Heat 1 tablespoon of the grapeseed oil in a large skillet over medium-high heat. Add the onions and bell peppers and a big pinch of salt to the pan and cook, stirring frequently, until they are tender, about 10 minutes. Transfer the onions and bell peppers to a bowl and set aside. Return the skillet to medium-high heat and add the remaining 1 tablespoon oil. Add the yuba to the hot pan and spread into a single layer. You want as much of the yuba touching the hot pan as possible so that it can brown and get kind of crackly. Using a spatula or tongs, flip the yuba so it continues to brown all over. Once nicely browned, transfer the yuba to another bowl. To serve, lightly toast the rolls on their cut sides. Mound about ½ cup yuba onto each roll. Top the yuba with some of the cooked onions and bell peppers. Smother everything with the hot pump cheese sauce.

NEW CREATION

SERVES 4

1 cup Chickpea Mayo
(page 211)

2 tablespoons Dijon mustard

1½ teaspoons maple syrup

4 small potato rolls, split in half

Grapeseed oil

2 cups Marinated Yuba Strips
(see page 210)

12 dill pickle slices

Mix together the mayo, mustard, maple syrup, and a substantial pinch of black pepper in a medium bowl. Set the sauce aside. In a large dry skillet, toast the rolls on the cut sides until just a little browned. Arrange the rolls wide open on a plate.

Heat a few tablespoons of grapeseed oil in a large skillet over medium-high heat. Add the yuba and cook, flipping and stirring frequently, until it is a little crispy and brown on most pieces but still has some gooey areas as well. Using tongs or a spatula, divide the yuba among the rolls. Spoon as much or as little of the sauce as you like over the yuba. It is fine if it breaches the edge of the sandwich and pools a little bit on the plate. Top each sandwich with 3 pickle slices and eat. This is also good without a bun—a common request—with the griddled yuba, sauce, and pickles in a small bowl.

UPTOWN

MAKES 4 SANDWICHES

1 medium yellow
  onion, chopped

2 tablespoons grapeseed oil

1 pound firm tofu, crumbled

½ cup tamari mixed with
  ½ cup water

AMERICAN SAUCE

1 medium yellow onion, cut
  into medium dice

1 butternut squash, cut into
  medium dice

2 russet potatoes, cut into
  medium dice

2 carrots, cut into medium dice

2 tablespoons raw sugar

1 tablespoon Dijon mustard

½ cup white wine vinegar

½ cup nutritional yeast flakes

4 soft hoagie rolls

4 cups shredded
  iceberg lettuce

8 tomato slices

2 cups sliced pickles

1 cup Spicy Mayo (page 212)

Running a restaurant is a constant struggle to retain employees. This sandwich was the brainchild of Dominic, one of our finest ex–burger wrappers, who was eventually poached by one of the SB partners for another business. Talk about skullduggery! This is a very loose interpretation of a chopped cheese, a bodega specialty commonly found in the Bronx and Harlem, and it is messy and utterly satisfying. Dominic, a vegan kid from Connecticut, has never had the real version; he just impresario-ed it together from NYC lore, Malcolm McLaren style.

Sauté the onion in the grapeseed oil in a skillet on high heat until charred around the edges, about 5 minutes. Add the tofu and cook until browned. Deglaze the pan with the tamari mixture and set aside.

To make the American sauce, in a Dutch oven over high heat, add the diced onion and cook, stirring constantly, until caramelized, about 10 minutes. Add the squash, potatoes, and carrots and cover with water. Cook, uncovered, until all of the vegetables are soft and falling apart. Strain off but reserve any liquid. In batches in a blender, process the vegetable mixture, thinning it out with the reserved cooking liquid as necessary. You want a thick yet pourable puree, reminiscent of an American cheese sauce. Season with salt and pepper, and add the sugar, mustard, vinegar and yeast flakes.

In a clean skillet, reheat the tofu mixture and stir in some of the "cheese" sauce, tossing it together with the tofu just until bubbling and hot. Scoop this (very messy and loose) mixture onto a toasted roll. Top with more sauce, shredded lettuce, slices of tomato, pickles, and spicy mayo. Serve immediately with lots of napkins.

SATURATED PARTY SUB

MAKES 1 LOAF

1 loaf hearty sesame
semolina bread

½ cup Oregano Vinaigrette
(page 62)

½ cup golden balsamic vinegar

¼ cup Dijon mustard

1 cup sliced pickles

1 cup shredded carrots

5 Medjool dates, chopped

3 cups chopped romaine lettuce

½ cup chopped pickled
cherry peppers

½ cup scallions, shredded
and charred

1 cup torn Castelvetrano olives

2 cups Hammered
Mushrooms (page 207)

1 cup Bread and Butter
Cauliflower (page 54)

1 eggplant, thickly sliced
and roasted

½ cup Chickpea Mayo
(page 211)

We spent a lot of time as kids with half-eaten halves of things wrapped in foil in our coat pockets: SF Mission burritos, elusive San Diego Faque burgers, Subway Veggie Delite hoagies. The true test of the foodstuff always being how it held up (or sometimes even got better) with a five-hour room-temperature in-the-pocket marination. Get a nice sturdy loaf for this one, soak the heck out of it, pack it full of vegetables, wrap it in plastic, and then weigh it down overnight in the fridge. The end result is a terrinelike slab that's sliceable, juicy, no longer a sandwich, and terrific to eat.

Slice the loaf of bread in half and scoop out some of the innards (you can reserve this bread to make bread crumbs for another recipe). Lay the bread out on a cutting board and soak the insides liberally with oregano vinaigrette, golden balsamic vinegar, and mustard. Pile all of the vegetables listed on top of the bread—it should look overloaded and out of control. Season with salt and black pepper, and squirt the top with the mayo. Place the top on and tightly wrap in plastic wrap. Place in the refrigerator, put a heavy weight on the sub (for example, a cast-iron skillet), and allow it to rest overnight. The next day slice it into strips while the plastic is still on. Serve ice cold or gently warm one side of a slice in a cast-iron griddle.

PASTRAMI-SPICED TOFU ON RYE WITH GRIDDLED ONIONS

SERVES 4

2 medium yellow onions,
   shredded on a mandoline
Extra virgin olive oil
2 tablespoons tamari mixed
   with 2 tablespoons water
1 recipe Pastrami Tofu
   (page 208)
8 slices rye bread
2 cups American Sauce
   (page 40)

Boring old plain tofu gets a *Lou Reed-Transformer* makeover with a piquant wet spice rub that exfoliates and permeates the bean curd innards into something wholly new. The griddled onion condiment has a beefy aroma while utilizing no creepy tactics to get it that way. Search out some middle-of-the-road sliced New York deli rye (no rugged Nordic rabble-rouser loaves need apply here) and this bastardization of three or four different sandwiches will prove to be quite satisfying.

Make the griddled onions first. Cook the onions with a little bit of olive oil in a heavy saucepan over high heat until deeply caramelized and brown. Season with salt and pepper, deglaze with the tamari mixture, and keep cooking until very dark (think French onion soup). Reserve. In a separate cast-iron skillet, sear slabs of spice-rubbed tofu until golden brown and caramelized. To serve, toast the rye bread, then top with the onions and 2 slices each of the tofu. Pour on an overwhelming amount of the sauce, top with another slice of the toasted rye, press together, and eat immediately.

Cool
Salads

BURNT BROCCOLI SALAD

This was our first salad. It's on the main menu and never leaves. There are multiple steps, but the end result is worth it. Initially it was a fish sauce–less take on a Thai-style green papaya salad that strayed so far from the original it no longer resembled anything remotely stolen. A very dry cast-iron skillet on high heat will burn your broccoli nicely (no oil though, as it will ignite immediately).

CORIANDER VINAIGRETTE

MAKES 2 CUPS

2 tablespoons coriander
   seeds, toasted
¼ cup water
½ cup seasoned rice
   wine vinegar
Juice of 1 lime
½ cup extra virgin olive oil

Finely grind the coriander seeds in a spice grinder, coffee grinder, or mortar and pestle. Mix the ground-up seeds with the water in a medium bowl. Add the rice wine vinegar and lime juice and mix to combine. Slowly whisk in the olive oil.

EGGPLANT PUREE

MAKES 2 CUPS

2 Japanese eggplants
¼ cup extra virgin olive oil,
   plus more for drizzling
2 tablespoons malt vinegar
1 tablespoon maple syrup
1 tablespoon smooth tahini

Preheat the oven to 375°F.

Cut the eggplants in half lengthwise and place on a baking sheet with the skin directly touching the pan. Drizzle a little olive oil over the inner flesh and season with a little salt and pepper. Cook the eggplants in the oven until lightly browned and fully tender, about 30 minutes. Let cool.

Put the eggplants, including the skin, into the bowl of a food processor (or use an immersion blender). Add the malt vinegar, maple syrup, and tahini to the bowl. With the motor running, stream in the olive oil. Add salt and pepper as needed. If the puree is too thick, add a little water and blend a bit more.

continues

CANDIED CASHEWS

MAKES 2 CUPS

2 cups roasted
  unsalted cashews

3 tablespoons simple syrup

½ cup turbinado sugar

1 teaspoon kosher salt

Preheat the oven to 325°F. Line a baking sheet with parchment paper.

Toss the cashews with the simple syrup in a medium bowl until lightly coated. There should not be liquid in the bottom of the bowl. Sprinkle the sugar and salt all over the nuts and toss to coat. Spread the nuts out into a single layer on the baking sheet. Bake until the cashews begin to toast and the sugar becomes glossy, about 15 minutes. Let cool and roughly chop. This method of simple syrup and turbinado sugar and salt can be used for candying just about anything—sunflower seeds, coconut, corn chips . . .

BURNT BROCCOLI SALAD

SERVES 6

2 bunches broccoli, florets
  separated from the stems,
  stems peeled and shaved
  lengthwise on a mandoline

2 Fresno chiles, cut in half
  lengthwise, seeded, and
  thinly sliced

1 tablespoon cane sugar

1 teaspoon kosher salt

½ cup white wine vinegar

Fresh cilantro leaves

Heat a dry medium cast-iron skillet over high heat. Cook the broccoli florets, tossing occasionally, until the surfaces are blackened, 10 to 15 minutes. Transfer to a large plate and let cool.

Toss the chiles, sugar, and salt in a small bowl. Let sit for a few minutes, until the juices release, then add the white wine vinegar.

To serve, toss the charred broccoli florets, the broccoli stems, and ½ cup of the coriander vinaigrette in a large bowl. Serve over the eggplant puree topped with chopped candied cashews, cilantro leaves, and drained Fresno chiles.

TAHINI RANCH ROMAINE SALAD

SERVES 6

TAHINI RANCH DRESSING

1 cup smooth tahini
   (we use Soom)

½ cup water

½ cup fresh lemon juice

⅓ cup each chopped fresh flat-
   leaf parsley, dill, and chives

½ teaspoon garlic powder

2 tablespoons maple syrup

1 tablespoon extra virgin olive oil

BREAD AND BUTTER
CAULIFLOWER

1 head cauliflower, cut into
   small florets

2 cups cider vinegar

1½ cups cane sugar

3 tablespoons kosher salt

1 green bell pepper,
   thinly sliced

1 medium red onion,
   thinly sliced

1 ripe avocado,
   pitted and skin removed

3 heads romaine lettuce, cut
   into 1-inch pieces

1 English cucumber, cut into
   medium dice

Nice olive oil

Our pastry chef used to work for a guy who claimed that all anyone really wants when they go out to eat is a steak and a Caesar salad. This guy is kind of a knucklehead, but he might be right, at least about the Caesar salad part. This is our vegan version. It's as salty as a bag of pretzels and, we like to think, as satisfying as a rib eye.

For the tahini ranch dressing, mix the tahini, water, and lemon juice in a bowl until smooth. Add more water if needed to get a smooth consistency. Add the chopped herbs, garlic powder, and maple syrup, and season with salt and black pepper. Ideally, let sit overnight to allow the flavors to come together.

For the bread and butter cauliflower, put the florets in a large bowl or heat-safe container with at least 2 inches of room at the top. Combine the cider vinegar, sugar, and salt in a saucepan. Add the sliced bell peppers and onions to the saucepan and bring to a boil over high heat. Once boiling, pour the liquid—including the peppers and onions—over the cauliflower. Check the seasoning for salt and sugar. Let sit for at least 30 minutes before using. These will stay good refrigerated for a couple weeks.

To assemble the salad, smash up the avocado in the bottom of a large bowl. Add the romaine, a handful of cauliflower, the chopped cucumbers, a splash of olive oil, a splash of the cauliflower pickling liquid, and salt and black pepper. Using your hands, toss the lettuce so that the leaves are well coated with avocado-y goo. Serve with little dots of the ranch dressing. It doesn't need too much.

CARAWAY SLAW

SERVES 6

CARAWAY VINAIGRETTE

2 teaspoons Dijon mustard

1 tablespoon maple syrup

1 cup cider vinegar

2 tablespoons caraway seeds, toasted and partially ground

1½ cups grapeseed oil

1 head green cabbage, shredded

2 teaspoons kosher salt

2 teaspoons cane sugar

2 carrots, shredded

2 celery stalks, cut into small dice

2 scallions, thinly sliced

4 juicy dates

¼ cup unsweetened coconut flakes, toasted

¼ cup toasted rye bread crumbles

This is our version of a carrot and raisin salad, the type found at the pickle bar at the Silver Spring, MD, inimitable Parkway Deli. There's sweetness in the form of hacked-up dates and an underlying breadiness from the caraway vinaigrette. You can make it in advance and just let it stew in its own juices, flicking the dry stuff on top at the last minute.

For the caraway vinaigrette, mix together the mustard, maple syrup, cider vinegar, and a good pinch of salt in a bowl. Add the caraway seeds. Drizzle in the grapeseed oil while whisking. Add more salt if needed. This dressing should be quite acidic.

Toss the cabbage with the salt and sugar in a large bowl. Transfer the cabbage to a large colander set over a bowl and let drain for at least 30 minutes. Rinse the cabbage with cold water and wring it out in a clean dish towel until very dry. Transfer to a large mixing bowl. Add the carrots, celery, and scallions to the bowl and toss to combine. Remove the pits from the dates—if they have pits—and tear the dates into small pieces while adding them to the slaw mix. Dress with the caraway vinaigrette, salt, and pepper. Serve topped with a sprinkle of toasted coconut and rye bread crumbles.

CHICORIES SALAD

SERVES 6

3 heads chicory greens (such
as Castelfranco, radicchio,
endive, or frisée)

½ head green cabbage,
shredded

2 nice tart apples, such as
Granny Smith, thinly sliced

Pickled Red Onions (page 204)

Caraway Vinaigrette (page 56)

1 cup toasted chopped almonds

Campo Rosso Farm, based in Pennsylvania, is owned by Jessi Okamoto and Chris Field. They sell their vegetables at New York City's Union Square farmers' market only on Fridays, and while their tomatoes in July are unfathomably perfect, the chicories (Castelfranco, radicchio, endive, frisée) that fill their table during the autumn months are better than anything we've ever had (even in Friuli). The couple is a little weird (in a good way) and slightly psychotic about the vegetables they grow, so we became fast buddies right when Superiority opened up. This salad utilizes the same caraway vinaigrette as the previous slaw, but is balanced differently by the cough syrup–like bitterness of the chicory leaves. This one is very easy.

Chop up the chicories into about 1-inch pieces and put into a large bowl along with the cabbage. Toss in the apples and a small handful of the pickled onions. Dress with the caraway vinaigrette and season with salt and pepper. Serve with some toasted almonds on top.

GREEN BROWN RICE WITH YELLOW BEETS

SERVES 4

GREEN DRESSING

4 scallions, cut into
½-inch pieces

2 cups fresh Thai basil leaves

1 cup fresh Italian basil leaves

1½ cups fresh mint leaves
(shiso is nice too, if it's
available)

1 cup fresh flat-leaf parsley
(stems are fine)

1½ cups Chickpea Mayo
(page 211)

3 large yellow beets, peeled
and cut into 1-inch cubes

Extra virgin olive oil

1 cup seasoned rice
wine vinegar

Juice of 2 limes

2 cups cooked
brown rice (page 211)

Crushed red pepper flakes

½ cup marcona almonds,
toasted and chopped

Fresh Thai basil/Italian
basil/mint

A lot of things in life prove the adage that the sum is greater than its parts. *Spaghetti al pomodoro*, the 1983 Baltimore Orioles, the first couple Devo records, the cast of *The Jerk*, a good 3 a.m. NYC deli BLT, these all come to mind. This salad pops up almost too much on our specials board. There's an illegitimate green goddess dressing that flirts with a pesto milieu while staying very much on the outskirts, and yellow beets that flagrantly ignore their inherent earthiness. If you can find some Thai basil to throw on top, its usual cinnamony quality will be downplayed by the other components in a sum that is greater than the parts.

To make the green dressing, either in a very hot dry pan or under the broiler, char the scallions until deeply browned and tender. Set aside to cool off. In a food processor or with an immersion blender, blend all the herbs with the mayo and charred scallions until a smooth dressing forms. Thin with water if needed. Season with salt and black pepper.

Preheat the oven to 375°F. Line a baking sheet with parchment paper.

Toss the beets with a little olive oil, salt, and black pepper and spread out into a single layer on the baking sheet. Bake the beets until they are tender and begin to brown a little at their edges, 20 to 30 minutes. While the beets are in the oven, mix together the rice wine vinegar and lime juice in a medium bowl. Once the beets are done, immediately toss them while they are very hot into the vinegar mixture. Let them sit for at least 30 minutes.

In a medium bowl, gently mix together brown rice, ¼ to ½ cup green dressing, and a big pinch of red pepper flakes until the rice is well dressed. Add the drained pickled beets and a tablespoon or two of the beet pickling liquid to the bowl and stir to combine. Top with the chopped marcona almonds and scatter torn bits of basil and mint over everything. Serve at room temperature or, if on a particularly hot day, slightly chilled.

CHOPPED SALAD

SERVES 6

OREGANO VINAIGRETTE

2 garlic cloves

3 tablespoons nice
   dried oregano

Juice of 2 lemons

⅔ cup red wine vinegar

1¼ cups extra virgin olive oil

ROASTED CHICKPEAS

One 15-ounce can
   chickpeas, drained

2 tablespoons
   extra virgin olive oil

3 tablespoons tomato sauce

1 tablespoon red wine vinegar

2 teaspoons smoked paprika

1 teaspoon Korean chile flakes

1 tablespoon fennel
   seeds, toasted

1 tablespoon nutritional
   yeast flakes

1 tablespoon fennel
   seeds, toasted

2 garlic cloves, minced

1 head iceberg lettuce,
   shredded

2 small heads radicchio,
   thinly sliced

¾ cup Hammered Mushrooms
   (page 207)

¼ cup sliced pepperoncini

¼ cup Pickled Golden Raisins
   (page 205)

¼ cup sliced
   Castelvetrano olives

The inner workings of this salad were blatantly ripped off of the chopped salad served at Pizzeria Mozza in Los Angeles. However, by eliminating the cured shredded meat and provolone cheese, and tweaking Nancy Silverton's masterpiece of a dish into something totally vegan, we feel strongly that this is not out-and-out robbery. Lawyers will have to hash this one out in a boardroom somewhere.

For the oregano vinaigrette, put the garlic, oregano, and lemon juice in a blender and blend on high until everything is pulverized. Add the red wine vinegar and salt and black pepper and blend to combine. With the blender running, stream in the olive oil.

Preheat the oven to 325°F. Lightly grease a baking sheet with olive oil.

To make the roasted chickpeas, toss the chickpeas with the olive oil, tomato sauce, red wine vinegar, paprika, chile flakes, yeast flakes, fennel seeds, garlic, and salt and black pepper in a medium bowl. Check the seasoning—the mixture should be intensely seasoned. Spread the chickpeas into a single layer on the baking sheet. Bake until the chickpeas are mostly dry on the outside but still tender on the inside, 35 to 40 minutes. Let cool.

Mix together the iceberg lettuce and radicchio in a large salad bowl. Add the mushrooms, pepperoncini, raisins, olives, and chickpeas and toss, making sure to disperse every component evenly. Right before serving, dress the salad with the oregano vinaigrette—4 tablespoons or so—and season with salt and black pepper if needed. Serve immediately.

VARIATION

ANTIPASTO PASTA SALAD

For a more substantial version of this salad, add a 1-pound box of cooked and cooled pasta (we use De Cecco gnocchi shape, but shells or penne would work nicely) to the lettuce mix. The rest of the assembly is the same.

WEDGELESS WEDGE SALAD

SERVES 4 TO 6

WEDGELESS DRESSING
1 cup tahini
Juice of 2 lemons
½ cup water
1½ teaspoons maple syrup
½ teaspoon toasted sesame oil

1 head iceberg lettuce, cut
   into irregular bite-size
   triangles
½ cup Roasted Red Tomatoes
   (page 71)
½ cup Hammered Mushrooms
   (page 207)
Chopped fresh flat-leaf parsley

A wedge salad is always pretty okay in our book. This is our version, and, surprise, yes, it's void of animal products (imagine that). We also shred the iceberg rather than gobbing a dressing to run down all over a quarter hunk of compacted lettuce. Mushrooms are the bacon and the tomatoes are the tomatoes.

For the wedgeless dressing, mix the tahini, lemon juice, and water in a bowl until smooth. Add more water if needed to get a smooth dressing. Add the maple syrup and sesame oil. Season with salt and pepper.

To assemble the salad, arrange the iceberg lettuce in a heap on a plate. Scatter the tomatoes and mushrooms evenly over the lettuce. Drizzle liberally with wedgeless dressing and a fistful of parsley.

HOME-STYLE POTATO SALAD

SERVES 6

1 pound russet potatoes, peeled
and cut into 1-inch pieces

2 tablespoons plus 1 teaspoon
cane sugar

2 tablespoons white
wine vinegar

2 tablespoons seasoned rice
wine vinegar

1 English cucumber, cut into
small dice

2 to 3 cups green peas, fava
beans, cut snap peas, and/or
string beans, blanched

1½ cups Chickpea Mayo
(page 211)

1 cup fresh chervil, finely
chopped, plus a little extra
for garnish

2 scallions, thinly sliced

The key here is to use normal commodity potatoes (no market fingerlings, nothing waxy), and the presence of vinegar to miraculously and scientifically keep the chopped russets intact while getting semi-violently boiled. We do a version of this throughout the year, but when you can get your paws on springtime farmers' market chervil that will make your rented taxi or backseat stink of licorice, then you have really gotten the point of this book.

Put the potatoes into a large pot. Add 2 quarts cold water, 2 tablespoons salt, 2 tablespoons of the sugar, and the white wine vinegar to the pot and bring to a boil over high heat. Once the liquid is boiling, reduce the heat a little and cook until the potatoes are just tender—they should still hold their shape—about 10 minutes. Drain in a colander and immediately transfer to a baking sheet, spreading the potatoes into a single layer. Sprinkle the hot potatoes with the rice wine vinegar and set aside to cool completely.

Meanwhile, in a large bowl, toss diced cucumber with the remaining 1 teaspoon sugar and a good pinch of salt. Once the potatoes are cool, add to the bowl with the cucumbers. Also add the green vegetables of your choice (note: you can use all of one kind or a variety—frozen peas work nicely here too). Mix in the mayonnaise, chervil, scallions, and 1 teaspoon pepper and stir until the potatoes are fully coated in an herby creamy sauce. Cover the bowl with plastic wrap and let sit in the refrigerator for at least 30 minutes—though a little longer is often better—to allow the flavors to blend together. Remove from the refrigerator 15 minutes before serving—it will taste better. Check seasoning for salt and acid. If needed, add more salt and a splash more rice wine vinegar. Top with chopped chervil and freshly ground pepper.

CORN AND TOMATOES WITH BRUISED BASIL AND OLIVE OIL CROUTONS

SERVES 4

CREAMLESS
CREAMED CORN

6 ears of corn, husked, kernels
    removed from the cob,
    cobs saved

Grapeseed or extra virgin
    olive oil

1 medium yellow onion, cut
    into small dice

Nice olive oil

6 nice ripe tomatoes,
    red or green

2 tablespoons extra virgin
    olive oil

3 tablespoons seasoned rice
    wine vinegar

2 teaspoons Korean chile flakes

1 cup picked fresh basil leaves

½ cup toasted
    sourdough croutons

Save this one for when you are cranking the AC down to 64, your hair is curling uncontrollably, and everyone is yammering on about the humidity. Deep summer. When the corn is sweeter than the draped sauce on a turnpike Cinnabon, and the tomatoes require little more than responsible salting and a squirt of olive oil. It helps that the fronds of basil at the market at this same time are cunning and laserlike in their perfect basility.

To make the creamless creamed corn, bring 2 quarts of water to a boil in a large pot. Add the 6 reserved corncobs and let them boil for 20 to 30 minutes. Remove and discard the cobs but save the liquid—this is corn stock. In a deep skillet over medium-high heat, add a few table-spoons of grapeseed oil. Add the diced onion along with a large pinch of salt and cook, stirring very frequently, until the onions develop a dark brown color and stick to the bottom of the pan a little bit. Add the corn kernels and cook for 1 minute more. Add 3 cups of the corn stock to the pot and reduce the heat to medium-low. Using a spoon, scrape the stuck brown bits off the bottom of the pot. Cook everything until the kernels are just tender, 10 to 15 minutes, then remove from the heat. Using an immersion blender, blend the corn mixture—it should be pretty chunky, like loose polenta. Season with a splash of nice olive oil, salt, and pepper and let cool to room temperature.

To assemble, cut the tomatoes into large chunks that still can be eaten in one bite. Combine the tomatoes with the olive oil, rice wine vinegar, chile flakes, and salt and pepper in a medium bowl. Stir gently to combine. Tear the basil leaves and smear them together to release their oils. Add to the bowl and toss one more time. To serve, put 2 cups creamed corn on the bottom of a serving dish and top with the tomatoes and a little bit of their liquid. Finish with nice olive oil and a few croutons (not too many—let the tomatoes be the star).

ROASTED RED TOMATOES WITH CREAMLESS CREAMED CORN

SERVES 4

Any leftover tomatoes or not-
so-great tomatoes, cut into
large chunks

2 tablespoons extra virgin
olive oil

1 to 2 tablespoons raw sugar

2 teaspoons
crushed red pepper flakes

2 teaspoons fennel seeds,
toasted and crushed, plus
more for garnish (optional)

2 garlic cloves, thinly sliced

2 cups Creamless Creamed
Corn (page 70)

1 cup picked fresh basil leaves

2 tablespoons red wine vinegar

Grilled bread drizzled with olive
oil to serve

Preheat the oven to 300°F.

Combine the tomatoes, olive oil, sugar, red pepper flakes, fennel seeds, and garlic in a shallow baking dish. Add some salt and be generous with black pepper. Stir to combine and put into the oven. Cook for as long as possible, 1 to 2 hours, until the tomatoes break down some and the tomato liquid concentrates and becomes thicker. To serve, mix the roasted tomatoes and some of their liquid with the corn, tear in the basil leaves, add some red wine vinegar, and season with salt and black pepper. You can add more toasted and slightly ground fennel seeds if you want. Serve with hot grilled/toasted bread drizzled with olive oil. Use your bread to scoop up the tomato-corn gloop.

ICE-COLD HERBED MELON AND CUCUMBER SALAD

SERVES 6

6 cups melon cut into 1½-inch
  pieces (avoid the seeds)
2 English cucumbers, cut into
  1-inch pieces or smashed
  (see Iced and Smashed
  Cucumber Salad, page 84)
1 cup fresh Thai basil,
  roughly chopped
1 cup fresh cilantro,
  roughly chopped
1 cup fresh mint,
  roughly chopped
Zest and juice of 4 limes
1 tablespoon Korean
  chile flakes
1 to 2 teaspoons maple syrup

More summery bluster here. This straddles the line between salad and dessert. There are no alliums, so it could go either way. Keep everything very cold and it will be wholly refreshing and more satisfyingly hydrating than one of those curved aseptic boxes of coconut water or a plastic-bottled, fitness-club-vending-machine sports elixir.

Before you start, have this in mind: Try to keep everything as cold as possible. This salad is best eaten on a hot day either right out of the refrigerator or held on ice. Combine the melon and cucumber pieces in a large bowl. Add the herbs and gently toss so that all the herbs stick to the melon and cucumber pieces. Add the lime zest, lime juice, chile flakes, and a good amount of salt and mix well but gently. It may need more salt. The optimal flavor of the melon and cucumber relies on being highly salted. Add a pinch of pepper and taste. If necessary to smooth out the acidity of the lime or sweeten the melon, add a teaspoon or two of maple syrup. Refrigerate for at least 30 minutes before serving. Eat ice cold.

FENNEL AND CELERY SALAD WITH SPICY PEANUT SAUCE

SERVES 6

PEANUT SAUCE

One 16-ounce jar creamy
   peanut butter
1 cup pickled chile peppers
   (we use pickled Fresnos
   from the Burnt Broccoli
   Salad, page 50)
2 tablespoons pickling liquid
   from the peppers above
2 teaspoons maple syrup

3 fennel bulbs, shaved thinly
   on a mandoline
8 celery stalks, cut ¼ inch
   thick on a bias
Juice of 2 lemons
Extra virgin olive oil
1 small bundle fresh chives,
   cut thinly
½ cup dark raisins
½ cup unsalted roasted
peanuts, chopped

Once when we were listening to an AM talk radio show in the early 90s, Conservative host G. Gordon Liddy claimed on air that the word "crispy" was a fabrication of fast-food establishments like KFC and that "crisp" is the proper word. This salad is very crisp. Almost crispy.

To make the slightly spicy peanut sauce, place the peanut butter, chiles, and pickling liquid in the bowl of a food processor. Process until the chiles are totally chopped up and incorporated into the peanut butter. While the machine is running, stream in water until the sauce is pretty loose—the consistency of salad dressing. The peanut butter will look weird and seem to have separated. Keep adding water little by little and it will come back together and thin out. Add the maple syrup and salt to taste.

In a large mixing bowl, toss together the fennel and celery. Add the lemon juice and a splash of olive oil along with a substantial pinch of salt and black pepper. Stir in the chives and raisins. Drizzle with 1 cup of the peanut sauce right before serving and sprinkle with the chopped peanuts.

OKRA RICE SALAD

SERVES 6

OKRA RUB

1 cup firmly packed dark
    brown sugar

¾ cup smoked paprika

¼ cup raw sugar

⅓ cup kosher salt

3 tablespoons onion powder

3 tablespoons garlic powder

3 tablespoons chile powder

3 teaspoons freshly ground
    black pepper

1 to 3 teaspoons cayenne
    pepper (add as much or as
    little to taste)

2 teaspoons dry mustard

1 pound okra, cut on the bias
    into ½-inch-thick slices

About 2 tablespoons extra
    virgin olive oil

1 head green cabbage, cut
    into ¼-inch ribbons

1 tablespoon cane sugar

1 large bunch fresh dill, finely
    chopped, plus dill sprigs
    for garnish

2 cups cooked brown
    rice (page 211), cooled

½ cup labne or vegan yogurt

2 tablespoons malt vinegar

1 cup blanched slivered
almonds, toasted

We use a lot of cabbage at the restaurant. It takes up a lot of space. Until you cook it, then it takes up no space. It's in this salad, but you almost don't notice it. During the summer of 2016 we were committed to conquering the piles of greenmarket okra that we had been weirdly scared of in years prior. This roasting method squelches the unpleasant slimy goo that most people associate with okra. The dressing is thinned-out labne and finds us again reaching into the pantry for our favorite brown rice. Toss the seasoned spicy okra with the dressed rice and you have eerily re-created a wholesome version of Cool Ranch Doritos.

For the okra rub, mix together everything from the rub list (dark brown sugar, smoked paprika, etc.) in a medium bowl. Store in a dry, cool spot for up to 2 months until ready to use.

Preheat the oven to 375°F. Line two baking sheets with parchment paper.

Put the okra into a large bowl and add a little of the oil—just enough to barely coat. Add ¾ cup of the spice rub and toss the okra thoroughly so that each piece is coated with some rub. Divide the okra between the baking sheets and spread into a single layer. Bake for 15 minutes and check to make sure the edges aren't browning too fast. If so, just toss the okra with a spatula and return it to the oven. Check every 5 minutes until the okra is a darker golden brown. Remove from the oven and let cool for a bit.

Combine the cut cabbage with the sugar and 2 large pinches of salt in a large bowl. Toss thoroughly and let sit for about 15 minutes, until the cabbage begins to weep and wilt. Drain. Add the chopped dill to the cabbage and mix. Add the rice to the bowl and toss to evenly distribute the cabbage into the rice. In a small bowl, mix the labne with the malt vinegar and a splash of water and mix to make a smooth dressing. Pour over the cabbage and rice and mix to fully incorporate. Add 2 big pinches of black pepper and check the salt content. When you are ready to eat, scoop a little rice into a bowl. Add a small handful of the okra, and add another spoonful of rice on top of the okra. Top with the almonds and some picked fresh dill sprigs.

ROASTED CAULIFLOWER WITH TAMARIND, SHISO, AND PEANUTS

SERVES 6

PATTY SPICE BLEND

4 tablespoons cumin seeds

4 tablespoons mustard seeds

2 tablespoons aniseeds

2 star anise

6 tablespoons
  coriander seeds

2 teaspoons allspice

3 teaspoons fenugreek

TAMARIND SAUCE

1 cup tamarind pulp
  concentrate

½ cup maple syrup

1 tablespoon tamari

¼ cup extra virgin olive oil

1 large head cauliflower, cut
  into medium florets

1 cup shiso leaves, roughly
  chopped (fresh mint works
  here as well)

½ cup unsalted roasted
  peanuts, chopped

This patty spice blend is good to have on hand. It was our attempt to reverse engineer the seasoning of the ubiquitous Jamaican beef patties that all the finest street-corner pizza parlors of the East Village keep at room temperature in glass cases next to the pre-cut pies. The tamarind mixture sweetens and is an all-around great dipping sauce (not bad on a dollar slice, actually). Shiso may not be traditional to a beef patty, but it adds an herbal electricity that makes this salad very bright and craveable.

For the patty spice blend, toast everything from the spice blend list in a large dry skillet until fragrant. Grind in a clean coffee grinder. Transfer to a small bowl. Store in a cool, dry place for up to 2 months until ready to use.

For the tamarind sauce, mix together the tamarind pulp, maple syrup, and tamari in a small bowl. Season with salt if needed.

Preheat the oven to 450°F. Lightly grease two baking sheets.

Mix together the olive oil and 6 tablespoons of the spice blend in the bottom of a large bowl. Add the cauliflower florets to the bowl and toss until the florets are fully coated in oil and spices. Divide the florets between the baking sheets and spread into a single layer. Sprinkle generously with salt. Put the sheets in the oven and bake for 20 minutes, then check. The florets should be brown and crispy at the edges and tender in texture. Scatter the cauliflower on a serving dish. Drizzle with 1 cup of the tamarind sauce, and scatter the shiso leaves and chopped peanuts judiciously over the cauliflower. Eat at room temperature.

RAW SWISS CHARD SALAD

ROASTED GARLIC
VINAIGRETTE

4 garlic cloves, unpeeled

½ cup golden balsamic
vinegar

2 tablespoons water

1½ cups extra virgin olive oil

2 teaspoons kosher salt

1 bunch Swiss chard, leaves
separated from the stems,
stems saved

Grapeseed oil

One 8-ounce block halloumi
cheese, cut into ½-inch
cubes (or Cheesy Brined
Tofu, page 207, for a vegan
alternative)

½ cup Pickled Onions
(page 204)

1 cup really nice fruit
(blackberries or sliced plums
work well)

While usually braised or hammered to within an inch of its life, Swiss chard is also very tasty raw when it is young and fresh at the summer markets. Choose tender leaves and reserve the stems for their supporting-player crunch. The vinaigrette has a base of roasted garlic that will make your kitchen smell incredible and remind you just how good slow-cooked garlic is. When blackberries or plums are potent, we recommend folding in a few to the finished dish for their jammy bursts. The griddled halloumi cheese makes the whole thing hearty and satisfying. Roasted garlic? Almost raspberry vinaigrette? Warm cheese? What is this? 1987? Yeah, maybe.

For the roasted garlic vinaigrette, roast the garlic cloves, still in their peels, wrapped in aluminum foil in a 350°F oven until totally tender and golden in color, about an hour. Squeeze the garlic out of their peels before using. In a blender, blend the roasted garlic with the golden balsamic vinegar and water until the garlic is totally dissolved into the vinegar. With the blender running on a low speed, slowly stream in the olive oil and add the salt.

Tear the chard leaves into easily eaten–size pieces. Cut the stems into ¼-inch pieces and store in a small bowl with very cold water. In a medium skillet, heat a splash of grapeseed oil until it is very hot. Sear the halloumi until browned and crispy on at least two sides. Transfer to a small bowl and set aside.

In a large bowl, toss the chard leaves, cut stems (drain off the cold water), and pickled onions with ¼ cup of the garlic vinaigrette until lightly coated—responsibly dressed. Season with salt and pepper. Mound the dressed leaves onto a large plate. Tuck pieces of fruit and cheese into the mound of salad, making sure some are visible. Eat quickly while the halloumi is still warm.

ICED AND SMASHED CUCUMBER SALAD

SERVES 6

2 pounds English or
    Persian cucumbers

Pinch of sugar

½ cup labne or vegan yogurt

Zest and juice of 2 limes

1 tablespoon seasoned rice
    wine vinegar

2 tablespoons extra virgin
    olive oil, plus more
    for drizzling

½ teaspoon freshly ground
    black pepper

1 jalapeño chile, minced

4 tablespoons honey or maple
    syrup (for the vegan version)

1 cup crushed sesame
    breadsticks

2 cups cooked brown rice
    (page 211), cooled

4 scallions, minced

One of our first really *special* specials. We wait until there are oddly shaped, twisted, and multicolored local cucumbers at the summer greenmarket before doing this one. The jalapeño-honey makes the whole thing unexpectedly spicy, and the smashed cucumbers bring a nice texturally swollen, watery chomp. If you close your eyes it almost tastes like chicken salad.

Rinse the cucumbers and pat dry. Cut crosswise into pieces about 4 inches long. Place the cucumbers in a plastic bag and seal. Use the end of a rolling pin to smash the cucumbers. They will begin to break into pieces. Do not obliterate. Break or slice diagonally into bite-size pieces if the pieces are too large. Place the cucumber pieces in a strainer and toss with a big pinch of salt and a big pinch of sugar. Place a plastic bag filled with ice on top of the cucumbers to serve as a weight and place the strainer over a bowl. Let drain for 15 to 30 minutes on the counter, or in the refrigerator until ready to serve, up to 4 hours.

Mix the labne, lime zest, lime juice, rice wine vinegar, olive oil, ½ teaspoon salt, and the pepper in a bowl. This mixture should taste fiercely acidic and quite salty; add salt and vinegar as needed. Keep refrigerated.

Combine the minced jalapeño and honey in a small bowl and stir well until smooth.

Toast the breadstick pieces in a toaster oven or skillet. Drizzle with olive oil and stir occasionally, until golden and crunchy.

When ready to serve, shake the cucumbers well to drain off any remaining liquid and transfer to a bowl. Add the brown rice. Drizzle lightly with olive oil and toss. Add the scallions and half of the labne dressing and toss gently. Keep adding dressing until the cucumbers and rice are well coated but not drowned. Serve immediately. For each serving, scoop a large spoonful of salad into a bowl, drizzle with the spicy honey, and sprinkle with a handful of sesame croutons.

VEGETABLE SALAD

2 cups lentils du Puy, rinsed
  and picked over

1 star anise

4 tablespoons extra
  virgin olive oil

2 tablespoons red
  wine vinegar

1 medium eggplant, cut into
  medium dice

1 cup frozen green peas,
  defrosted

1 to 2 cups chopped fresh
  herbs (equal parts fresh
  mint, cilantro, and Thai basil)

2 heads radicchio,
  thinly sliced

EGGPLANT BRINE

3 cups white wine vinegar

½ cup water

¼ cup sugar

Not the greatest name, we know. The quick-brined eggplant is both a revelation and kind of a custardy treat, and helps the lentils feel slightly less underappreciated. Go crazy with the herbs, and the radicchio is in there for a bitter adult romp. Don't bother with fresh peas, even if they are in season; their presence here is muted, so the frozen bag is just fine.

Put the lentils, star anise, and 1 teaspoon salt in a large saucepan and cover with water by 3 inches. Bring to a rolling boil, then reduce to a simmer and cook until the lentils are just tender, about 25 minutes. Drain well and put into a bowl. While the lentils are still hot, add 2 tablespoons of the olive oil, the red wine vinegar, and salt and pepper. Set aside to cool to room temperature.

While the lentils are cooking, preheat the oven to 375°F.

Bring brine ingredients to a boil in a small saucepot, season with salt and pepper. Add the eggplant pieces and simmer for a few minutes, just until they can be pierced with a knife. They will retain their form. Immediately drain the eggplant and lay out on a baking sheet to cool as quickly as possible.

In a medium bowl, combine the lentils with the cooked eggplant, green peas, herbs, and radicchio. Check the seasoning. If necessary, add more red wine vinegar, salt, and pepper. Serve at room temperature.

SWEET-AND-SOUR RED BEETS WITH CREAM CHEESE AND FRIED PRETZELS

SERVES 6

BEET SPRINKLE

½ teaspoon pretzel salt or
    coarse sea salt

1 teaspoon freshly ground
    black pepper

1 tablespoon crushed red
    pepper flakes

2 tablespoons turbinado sugar

½ cup pumpkin seeds,
    toasted and crushed a little

½ cup sesame seeds, toasted

1 pound red beets

2 cups red wine vinegar

½ to 1 cup maple syrup

1 cup pretzels, crushed into
    irregular pieces

¼ cup extra virgin olive oil

1 cup cream cheese or
    vegan cream cheese,
    softened slightly

½ jalapeño chile, minced

Fresh dill sprigs

We are blessed with amazing regulars at Superiority Burger. Some folks come almost every day and get the same thing. Some always want to see what new stuff we have lurking. Either way, we love them all dearly. They are our life's blood. Jim, one of the "What's new and cool?" regulars, got two orders of these one night when we got really enthusiastic and talked up this salad as a middle finger to the snoresville beets and goat cheese combo that occupies many modern menus—even going so far as to say that the seed sprinkle was inspired by our pet bird's food, and that the fried pretzels are the platonic version of pretzels. The next day we were like, "Hey, Jim! How were the beets?" And he responded deadpan and dead serious, "Too much beets." So, um, recommended if you like beets.

To make the beet sprinkle, mix together everything from the sprinkle list and store in a sealed container for up to 2 months until ready to use.

Preheat the oven to 350°F.

Coat the beets with a little bit of grapeseed oil. Wrap the beets individually or in groups (depending on their size) in aluminum foil. Place the wrapped beets on a baking sheet and cook until a fork can pierce the flesh easily with no resistance, about 1 hour for medium beets. Let the beets cool for a short period. While the beets are cooling, mix together the red wine vinegar and maple syrup and season with salt—should be quite sour with the syrup just to cut the vinegary-ness. As soon as the beets can be handled, remove the aluminum foil and rub the skins off using a clean kitchen towel or your fingers. Cut into medium chunks and put into the bowl. Pour the vinegar mixture over the hot beets and let sit for at least 1 hour. Once cool, store covered in the vinegar liquid in the refrigerator for up to 3 days until ready to use.

Combine the pretzels and olive oil in a small saucepan over medium heat. Stirring frequently, fry the pretzels until they are a rich golden brown. Use a slotted spoon to remove them from the oil and drain on a plate lined with paper towels. In a small bowl, mix together the cream cheese and jalapeño and season with salt and black pepper. For each serving, scoop a little of the jalapeño cream cheese into the bottom of a bowl. Spoon a portion of the marinated beets on top of the cream cheese, being careful not to add too much of the beet pickling liquid. Sprinkle with some of the beet sprinkle (use about ½ cup total) and crushed fried pretzels. Finish with some fresh dill.

KOHLRABI SLAW

SERVES 6

2 large kohlrabi, peeled,
   stems saved, shredded
   thinly on a mandoline (toss
   with lemon juice if not using
   immediately)

1 cup cider vinegar

1 tablespoon mustard seeds

2 tablespoons cane sugar

2 teaspoons kosher salt

1 cup Chickpea Mayo
   (page 211)

1 tablespoon fresh
   lemon juice

1 teaspoon maple syrup

1 tablespoon Dijon mustard

1 teaspoon freshly ground
   black pepper

2 sour green apples, sliced
   ⅛ inch thick either with a
   mandoline or by hand

½ cup fresh dill, chopped

1 cup walnuts, darkly toasted
   and crushed

Plastic Japanese mandolines are a godsend. They also can be a philosophical dilemma. Sure, they slice vegetables rapidly, and staring down at a bowl full of perfect strings of kohlrabi will get the alpha tendencies in your cooking personality fully aroused and chest thumping. Just promise us to be careful. Don't let your mind wander off while the shredding attachment is clipped into the holster. Stay focused, and you will be rewarded with a bright salad that is sinus clearing, gently sweet, and virtuously tasty.

Cut the kohlrabi stems into ¼-inch pieces and place in a small bowl. In a small saucepan, combine the cider vinegar, mustard seeds, sugar, and salt and bring to a boil over high heat. Once it is boiling, pour over the cut stems and let sit for at least 30 minutes.

In another small bowl, mix together the mayo, lemon juice, maple syrup, mustard, and pepper to make the dressing for the slaw. The flavor should be a little acidic, a little sweet with an underlying mustard flavor.

Place the shredded kohlrabi in a large bowl and add a few spoonfuls of the pickled stems—don't worry about the mustard seeds; they add a nice texture and flavor to the salad. Add the dressing, the sliced apples, and the chopped dill and mix well to coat and cover everything. Check to make sure there is enough salt, pepper, and lemon acidity—if not, adjust. Top with the crushed walnuts right before serving.

WILD RICE SALAD WITH CANDIED HIBISCUS

SERVES 6

2 teaspoons finely chopped
  fresh rosemary

Zest of 1 lemon

1 teaspoon fresh ginger,
  grated on the Microplane

Juice of 2 lemons

1 tablespoon maple syrup

½ cup extra virgin olive oil

2 sweet potatoes, peeled and
  cut into 1-inch cubes

Extra virgin olive oil

2 tablespoons dark
  brown sugar

2 teaspoons Korean
  chile flakes

1 cup wild rice, rinsed

2 cups cooked brown rice
  (page 211)

Squeeze of lemon (optional)

4 scallions, thinly sliced

1 cup dried hibiscus
  soaked overnight in 1 cup
  simple syrup

Wild rice gets a bad rap in the rice community. Probably because it ain't rice. It cooks weird, it looks weird, and species wise, it's a grass. It is often combined with real rice just to keep everyone from completely freaking out. Bloated reconstituted dried hibiscus is the icing on the cake here. There are also some sneaky roasted sweet potato chunks present, but just ducking down and staying out of the way.

Mix together rosemary, lemon zest, ginger, lemon juice, maple syrup, and olive oil to make the dressing. Season with salt.

Preheat the oven to 375°F.

Toss the sweet potato cubes with a little olive oil, the dark brown sugar, chile flakes, and salt and pepper. Spread into a single layer on a baking sheet. Cook until browned and tender, 25 minutes. Remove from the oven and set aside.

Cook the wild rice in 3 cups of salted water until tender, about 40 minutes. Drain off any excess water and transfer to a large bowl. Mix the brown rice into the wild rice. Add the dressing and let sit for about 10 minutes to allow the rice to absorb the dressing. Check the seasoning for salt and pepper. If it needs any more acid, add a squeeze of lemon. Stir in the cooked sweet potato and scallions, and top with the candied hibiscus.

STUFFED CABBAGE SALAD

SERVES 6

Extra virgin olive oil

1 pound Brussels sprouts, brown ends trimmed, cut in half

½ teaspoon celery seeds

1 cup Roasted Red Tomatoes (page 71)

1 tablespoon smoked paprika

1 tablespoon sweet paprika

2 tablespoons dark brown sugar

¼ cup red wine vinegar

2 teaspoons kosher salt

1 teaspoon freshly ground black pepper

¼ cup extra virgin olive oil

2 cups cooked brown rice (page 211), warm

1 cup Hammered Mushrooms (page 207), finely chopped

½ cup dates, pitted and torn into pieces

½ cup walnuts, toasted and roughly chopped

1 cup fresh flat-leaf parsley, roughly chopped

2 cups shredded green cabbage

Juice of 1 lemon

One of our first proclamations when SB opened up was that we would never cook with Brussels sprouts. Between the chances of screwing up the spelling (on the specials board, on in-house prep lists) and the wheat-pasted ubiquity of the mini brassica, we were dead set against ever using them. Then Charlie and Lana, two of our favorite farmers from upstate, arrived with some late-summer Brussels still on the stalk and still sprouting a glorious head of leaves. We fell hard for them. Despite the nearly two-and-a-half-foot trees, the yield ended up being about half a sheet pan of cooked veg. So we ran this special for only a day, and even though people say not using Brussels sprouts is crazy, it seems pretty all right by us.

Preheat the oven to 425°F. Lightly grease a baking sheet.

Toss the Brussels sprouts with a few teaspoons of olive oil, the celery seeds, and salt in a medium bowl. Transfer to the baking sheet and roast until crisp on the outside and tender on the inside, about 30 minutes. Remove from the oven and set aside until ready to use.

While the sprouts are in the oven, make the dressing. Combine the roasted tomatoes, smoked paprika, sweet paprika, dark brown sugar, red wine vinegar, salt, and pepper in the bowl of a food processor. Run until the roasted tomatoes are broken down and a cohesive sauce forms. While the machine is running, slowly stream in the olive oil.

To assemble the salad, place the brown rice in a large bowl. Add the Brussels sprouts and chopped mushrooms and toss to combine. Add a few spoonfuls of the dressing and stir thoroughly—you do not want to overdress the rice and make it soggy. If the salad needs more dressing, add cautiously. Gently stir in the dates and walnuts. In a separate bowl, mix the green cabbage with the parsley and lemon juice. Add a pinch of salt and pepper. Mound the cabbage and parsley salad on top of the rice right before serving.

HALF-WILTED ESCAROLE WITH CORN BREAD AND ROASTED APRICOTS

SERVES 6

½ recipe Corn Bread (page 211) made with chile flakes and black pepper

1 large head escarole, cut into bite-size pieces

3 garlic cloves, sliced paper thin with a mandoline

¼ cup extra virgin olive oil

2 tablespoons red wine vinegar

4 very ripe apricots, cut into 1-inch pieces and tossed with a little sugar and lemon juice

½ cup fresh flat-leaf parsley, roughly chopped

Panzanella, you charlatan. C'mon. Too easy. Totally rote. How about we start this exchange in late spring prior to the sticky, seedy summer tomatoes that just flaunt their effortless beauty? The greens are slightly wilted and bitter here, and the apricots are fresh off the tree, but desperately in need of a clumsy warmth to unlock their true character. The corn bread just completely falls apart, clinging granularly to everything.

Preheat the oven to 325°F.

Crumble the corn bread into small croutons and spread out onto a baking sheet. Toast in the oven until they brown just slightly and are lightly dried on the exterior, about 15 minutes. Let cool before using.

Separate the escarole into two groups: Place about three-quarters of the escarole in a large bowl and the other quarter in a medium bowl. In a small skillet, combine the sliced garlic and olive oil and heat over medium-low heat. Don't walk away from this for too long as you don't want the garlic to burn. Swirl the pan a little and once all the garlic has just turned golden brown, remove the pan from the heat and pour the hot oil over the smaller bowl of escarole. Let the escarole wilt from the heat of the garlic oil and cool down. Add the wilted escarole, along with the oil and garlic pieces, to the larger bowl of raw escarole. Toss to mix the two. Toss the leaves with the red wine vinegar and season with salt and pepper. Add the corn bread pieces and apricots and give it one last gentle mix. Serve with chopped parsley scattered over the top. Note: If the fruit is not totally ripe—not as juicy, sweet, and tart as it could be— it can be roasted in a 300°F oven to concentrate the flavor and release more juices. Just let the roasted fruit cool before adding it to the salad.

PEAS AND PESTO

SERVES 6

6 cups packed basil leaves

1 garlic clove

½ cup marcona
almonds, toasted and
roughly chopped

1 cup extra virgin olive oil

1 pound shell-shaped pasta
(we use gnocchi shape)

2 cups green peas, fresh or
frozen (if fresh, blanched)

Who're we to claim intellectual property on this one? This recipe wrote itself. This is the only time we are going to insist on freshly shelled peas that are straight from the greenmarket. Look for De Cecco gnocchi-shaped pasta. Its marsupial quality is key for the slam dunk of cuteness this dish will unleash.

Bring a pot of salted water to a rolling boil. Prepare an ice bath. Blanch the basil leaves for only 5 seconds, until they turn bright green. Using a strainer or a spider, remove the leaves from the water and immediately plunge them into the ice bath. Save the blanching water. Drain quickly and squeeze dry in a clean kitchen towel. Transfer the basil to a blender and add the garlic clove, almonds, and olive oil and puree until a smooth sauce forms. Transfer to a bowl and season with salt and pepper.

In the pot of boiling water, cook the pasta until just shy of al dente. Immediately strain in a colander and then spread out the pasta on two flat sheet trays to cool as quickly as possible.

Combine the cooked pasta with the pesto and peas in a large bowl. Toss thoroughly so that the pesto really thickly coats all the pasta (inside and out) and the peas begin to find their way into the cavities of the shells. If the sauce is too thick, a squirt of water will make it creamy. Check the seasoning for salt and pepper and serve immediately.

ROASTED RUTABAGA WITH BROWN RICE AND POMEGRANATE MOLASSES

SERVES 6

½ cup plain yogurt, labne, or vegan yogurt

2 tablespoons smooth tahini

Juice of 1 lemon

1 teaspoon maple syrup (optional)

½ cup pomegranate molasses

1 jalapeño chile, minced

2 large rutabagas, skin-on, whole

Extra virgin olive oil

2 cups cooked brown rice (page 211), warm or at room temperature

½ cup fresh cilantro (stems are okay), chopped

1 cup crushed toasted sesame breadsticks

This was a midseason swap out for the smashed cucumber salad that no longer had greenmarket availability. Rutabagas are one of the only things regularly available at NYC greenmarkets all winter long, and long-cooked, very much a set-it-and-forget-it culinary act. But once they are done and still warm, you can squeeze them and a NY strip ooze of jus will be released from their vesicles. We cube some and mix it with labne and brown rice, saving a portion to shave last minute on top for an accidental Comté and/or clothbound Cheddar trompe l'oeil.

Mix together the yogurt, tahini, and lemon juice in a medium bowl. Slowly add water, a tablespoon at a time, to make a loose and smooth dressing. Season with salt and black pepper and, if the tahini is particularly bitter, the maple syrup. In a small bowl, mix the pomegranate molasses with the minced jalapeño.

Preheat the oven to 375°F.

Using your hands, coat the rutabagas with olive oil and wrap in aluminum foil. Roast until a knife can easily pierce the rutabagas, about 2 hours, maybe more if the rutabagas are large. Allow to cool in the foil. Once cooled, carefully chop 1½ rutabagas into 1-inch cubes, reserving the uncut portion.

Mix together the brown rice and rutabagas in a large bowl. Gradually add the yogurt dressing, being cautious not to drown the rice. Check for salt and black pepper. If the mixture seems too thick or gluey, add about a tablespoon of water and it should smooth out and become creamy. Add the chopped cilantro. Using a mandoline, slice the remaining rutabaga in thin shards that resemble irregular hunks of cheese, then add on top of the rice mixture. To serve, drizzle with a little of the spicy pomegranate molasses and a handful of the crushed breadsticks. Serve at room temperature or a little warmer.

BITTER GREENS WITH GRAPEFRUIT, RE-TOASTED CORN CHIPS, AND HALLOUMI

SERVES 6

Zest and juice of 3 limes

2 tablespoons seasoned rice wine vinegar

½ cup extra virgin olive oil

Grapeseed oil

One 8-ounce block halloumi cheese, cut into ½-inch cubes

2 large heads bitter greens (escarole, frisée, endive, etc.), torn into pieces

2 grapefruits, peel and pith removed, cut into suprêmes or segments

1 jalapeño chile, sliced paper thin with a mandoline

1½ cups crushed yellow corn chips, briefly re-toasted

Grapefruit is the chief flavor here. As a vinaigrette, it makes the greens taste hauntingly adult, which is crucial because the corn chips drag the whole mess back down to a junior high cantina. Even though there is not a speck of pork, pineapple, or raw onion at play in this salad, you get gently seduced by whispers of *tacos al pastor*.

Combine the lime zest, lime juice, and rice wine vinegar in a medium bowl. Whisk in the olive oil and add salt and black pepper.

In a large skillet over medium heat, add a few tablespoons of grapeseed oil. When the oil is shimmering, add the halloumi cubes and sear, turning frequently, until they are golden brown on at least two sides. Transfer to a small bowl.

In a large bowl, combine the bitter greens with some of the lime dressing and season again. Gently mix in the grapefruit pieces, jalapeño, grilled halloumi, and corn chips, making sure to evenly disperse everything throughout the greens. This salad should be eaten immediately.

Warm
Vegetables

GRIDDLED BROCCOLI RABE

SERVES 4

1 bunch broccoli rabe,
trimmed of tough stems

Grapeseed oil

½ cup pickled ramps,
garlic scapes, or shallots
(see page 204)

Crushed red pepper flakes

Zest and juice of 1 lemon

Nice extra virgin olive oil

More often than not, we have found that when you travel to Italy (for work or, like, a honeymoon) you consume mostly pasta, pizza, and weird paper-thin shaved meat. It's great and all, but when we are on the tarmac at VCE, reeling, staring out the window and wanting to cleanse the gluten ka-blam and go back to normalcy, we often daydream about this warm salad. It's the thing we want to eat on a daily basis. A little bitter, sweet from the pickled shallots, salty, and hoveringly spicy, fibrous. Really gives you something to chew on. And unavailable in most trattorias, osterias, and/or ristorantes in Italia.

Bring a large pot of heavily salted water to a boil. Prepare an ice bath. Drop the broccoli rabe into the boiling water and cook for 1 minute. Remove from the boiling water and immediately plunge it into the ice bath. Once it is cooled, remove from the ice bath and dry well with a clean kitchen towel. Cut into 2-inch pieces. This can be used right away or packed up and refrigerated for a day or two.

Heat a slick of grapeseed oil in a heavy sauté pan over medium heat until shimmering. Add the pickled ramps and cook for 1 minute, until they just start to brown. Add the broccoli rabe and toss with the pickled ramps—the rabe is already cooked so this is just to warm it up and evaporate some of the water from blanching. Transfer everything from the sauté pan into a medium bowl. Add a good pinch of red pepper flakes and salt and pepper and toss to combine. Add the lemon zest and lemon juice. Top with a nice olive oil.

BLANCHED BROCCOLI RABE WITH ORANGE-FENNEL VINAIGRETTE

SERVES 4

1 bunch broccoli rabe,
trimmed of tough stems

ORANGE-FENNEL
VINAIGRETTE

Zest and juice of 1 orange

Zest and juice of 1 lemon

1½ teaspoons maple syrup

2 tablespoons fennel seeds,
toasted and slightly ground

½ cup extra virgin olive oil

2 teaspoons Korean
chile flakes

1 cup pecans, toasted
and chopped

¼ cup Chickpea Mayo
(page 211)

Blanch the broccoli rabe (as in the griddled broccoli rabe recipe above).

For the orange-fennel vinaigrette, combine the orange juice, lemon zest, lemon juice, and maple syrup (save the orange zest for garnish) in a bowl. Add the fennel seeds and slowly drizzle in the olive oil while whisking. Season with salt and black pepper

In a large bowl, toss the broccoli rabe (either at room temperature or slightly chilled) with the vinaigrette. Season with more salt and black pepper, the chile flakes, and a bit more lemon juice if it tastes flat. To serve, zigzag with chickpea mayo, sprinkle on the pecans, and dot with the reserved orange zest.

STUFFED GREEN PEPPERS WITH COCONUT AND ICEBERG

SERVES 4

2 tablespoons grapeseed oil

1 pound firm tofu, drained well and roughly crumbled

2 tablespoons golden balsamic vinegar

2 tablespoons extra virgin olive oil, plus more for drizzling

1 medium yellow onion, cut into small dice

2 garlic cloves, minced

3 ears of corn, husked and kernels removed from the cobs, or 2 cups creamed corn

One 13-ounce can full-fat coconut milk

4 to 6 green bell peppers

2 cups shredded iceberg lettuce

¼ cup unsweetened coconut flakes, toasted

1 celery stalk, cut into small dice

2 tablespoons seasoned rice wine vinegar

"Stuffed 'pep-pahs' tonight, we don't want to miss that."
—Line from the first denouement of the 1979 film *Over the Edge*.
The toasted coconut–iceberg garnish on this one is pivotal.

Heat the grapeseed oil in a deep sauté pan over medium-high heat until shimmering. Add the crumbled tofu and cook until golden brown all over, about 8 minutes. Add the golden balsamic vinegar and cook for a little longer to let the sugar in the vinegar caramelize. Scrape the tofu into a bowl and set aside.

Rinse out the sauté pan and return to medium heat. Add the olive oil, onion, and a pinch of salt to the pan and cook, stirring often, until a deep brown color develops. Add the garlic and cook for a minute more, until aromatic. Deglaze the pan with water if the onions are getting too brown and sticking to the bottom of the pan. Add the corn, coconut milk, and the cooked tofu. Let this simmer for about 15 minutes. Remove the pan from the heat and blend a little using either an immersion blender or a food processor. The mixture should have the consistency of thick chili. Add salt and black pepper as needed.

Preheat the oven to 375°F. Lightly oil an 8-by-8-inch baking dish.

Cut the bell peppers in half lengthwise, deseed using a little paring knife, and remove the stem if you are concerned about accidentally eating it. Stuff the peppers with the tofu mixture using a small spoon—use the back of the spoon to push the mixture into the pepper to fully fill it. Add enough filling to form a mound on top of the pepper. Pack the peppers as tightly as possible into the baking dish with the stuffed part facing upward. Drizzle a little olive oil on top of the peppers, cover with aluminum foil, and cook, covered, for 25 minutes. Crank the oven to 425°F and cook for another 15 minutes, until the filling is browned. Serve these at room temperature or warm. Though the peppers are good on their own, a small salad of iceberg lettuce, toasted coconut, celery, and rice wine vinegar scattered over the top of the peppers right before serving is a nice garnish.

CRUNCHY POTATOES

Say we are selling a ton of burgers on a blustery, chilly winter night, or a busy unseasonably balmy Saturday afternoon when there's a gag-reel matinee rock show in the band shell a block away in Tompkins, and the folks jamming up the counter have never been to Superiority Burger before, and there are several exasperated new customers who are clamoring for French fries at the register and protesting, "You really don't have fries?" There are five versions here: Cheesed (with pump cheese, a spicy cashew sauce), Exploded Pierogi (with green applesauce and a salsa verde), Mambo-Sauced (a Washington, DC, regional delicacy), Capered (with a lemony caper mayo), and Green Cream (with an avocado and griddled onion topping). And no, we don't have fries.

CHEESED CRUNCHY POTATOES

SERVES 6

1 cup ketchup

1 batch Crunchy Potatoes
(page 208)

2 cups Pump Cheese
(page 204), hot

6 scallions, thinly sliced

Layer the ingredients in the following order: some ketchup, potatoes, pump cheese, a little more ketchup, and scallions.

continues

GREEN CHILE AND RAW APPLESAUCE CRUNCHY POTATOES

GREEN CHILE SAUCE

8 fresh hatch green chiles or
   frozen roasted chiles
2 tablespoons grapeseed oil
2 medium yellow onions,
   finely chopped
4 garlic cloves, thinly sliced
2 teaspoons ground cumin
1 teaspoon dried oregano
½ cup fresh cilantro,
   finely chopped
Juice of 1 lemon

APPLESAUCE

6 very tart green
   apples, unpeeled
1 cup fresh lemon juice
3 tablespoons maple syrup

1 batch Crunchy Potatoes
   (page 208), hot
1 cup sour cream or vegan
   alternative
Fresh cilantro leaves (optional)

Preheat the oven to 450°F. Lightly grease a baking sheet.

For the green chile sauce, place the chiles on the baking sheet and roast until the skins are really browned—almost black, about 30 minutes. Remove from the oven and carefully put the hot peppers into either a paper bag or a bowl, covered in plastic wrap, and let them steam for about 10 minutes. They will be much easier to peel. Peel the skin off and remove as many seeds as possible.

Heat a few tablespoons of the oil in medium saucepan over medium-high heat. Add the onions and a large pinch of salt. Stirring often, let the onions get very brown, 8 to 10 minutes. Add the garlic, cumin, and oregano and cook for 1 minute more. Add the roasted chiles and just enough water to cover the peppers. Bring the mixture up to a boil and reduce the heat. Let it simmer for 15 minutes or so. Take the pan off the heat and stir in the cilantro. Blend with an immersion blender to create a chunky sauce. Add lemon juice and season with salt. Keep warm until ready to use.

To make the applesauce, cut the apples into 1-inch pieces and immediately transfer them to a medium bowl, adding just enough lemon juice to cover—this will both intensify the sourness of this sauce and keep the apples from browning. Move the apples and lemon juice to a blender and blend at medium speed to break down the apples. Season with the maple syrup. The applesauce should not be sweet—it should still be very sour but balanced just slightly by the maple. Refrigerate in a covered container for up to 2 days until ready to use.

In either a large serving dish or individual bowls, spoon half of the green chile sauce into the bottom of the dish and spread a little to create a base for the potatoes. Mound the potatoes on top of the sauce. Drizzle more green sauce on top of the potatoes. Dot with substantial dollops of sour cream and applesauce. Finish with a little freshly ground black pepper and cilantro leaves, if you like. Eat as soon as possible.

MAMBO-SAUCED CRUNCHY POTATOES

SERVES 6

MAMBO SAUCE
2 tablespoons tomato paste
One 2-inch knob fresh ginger,
   peeled and roughly chopped
1 cup pineapple juice
½ cup white wine vinegar
½ cup firmly packed dark
   brown sugar
½ cup ketchup
3 tablespoons tamari
2 teaspoons Frank's
   RedHot sauce

1 batch Crunchy Potatoes
   (page 208), hot
4 small sweet peppers, cut
   into ¼-inch rings
4 scallions, thinly sliced

For the mambo sauce, combine the tomato paste and ginger with about 1 cup water in a medium saucepan. Over medium heat, cook until all the water has evaporated and the tomato paste starts to brown. Add the pineapple juice and white wine vinegar and scrape the bottom of the pan thoroughly. Add the brown sugar, ketchup, tamari, and hot sauce. Bring to a boil, lower the heat, and cook until the liquid reduces almost by half and the sauce thickens, like sweet-and-sour sauce. In individual bowls, generously spoon the mambo sauce over the hot crunchy potatoes. Strategically place the sweet pepper rings on top of the potatoes and sprinkle with the scallions.

CRUNCHY POTATOES WITH CAPER SAUCE

SERVES 6

CAPER SAUCE
1 cup Chickpea Mayo
   (page 211)
Zest and juice of 2 lemons
½ cup capers packed in salt,
   rinsed and finely chopped
1 teaspoon maple syrup

1 batch Crunchy Potatoes
   (page 208), hot
Squeeze of lemon
½ cup fresh flat-leaf parsley,
   roughly chopped

For the caper sauce, mix together the mayo, lemon zest, lemon juice, capers, and maple syrup in a bowl. Season with salt and pepper. Thin with water if the sauce seems too thick—it should be loose enough to drizzle.

In individual bowls, spoon the caper sauce liberally over the hot crunchy potatoes. Finish with a squeeze of lemon and some chopped parsley. Very easy.

continues

CRUNCHY POTATOES WITH GREEN CREAM AND GRIDDLED ONIONS

SERVES 6

GREEN CREAM

2 very ripe avocados, pitted
    and skin removed
4 cups fresh cilantro leaves
    and stems, roughly chopped
1 cup fresh flat-leaf parsley
    leaves and stems,
    roughly chopped
1 garlic clove
Juice of 2 lemons
2 tablespoons extra
    virgin olive oil

2 medium red onions,
    thinly sliced
2 tablespoons grapeseed oil
1 batch Crunchy Potatoes
    (page 208), hot
4 cups shredded
    iceberg lettuce

Combine the avocados, cilantro, parsley, garlic, lemon juice, and olive oil in the bowl of a food processor and blend until smooth. Add salt and pepper to taste. If the consistency is too thick, add a little bit of water to bring it together.

Heat a large skillet over medium-high heat. Add a tablespoon or so of the grapeseed oil and once the oil is shimmering, add the red onions and a pinch of salt. Cook until the onions develop some nice caramelization and are slightly softened but still retain some texture, about 15 minutes. Transfer the onions to a small bowl.

Spoon some of the green cream onto the bottom of a serving dish. Mound the potatoes on top of that. Cover the potatoes in the rest of the green cream. Dot with grilled onions and finish with a mound of iceberg lettuce. Eat immediately.

BEAN TOAST

SERVES 6

3 cups dried or fresh beans
(a mix or one kind—gigante
beans are a good choice)

6 tablespoons extra virgin
olive oil, plus more for
splashing and drizzling

2 big fresh rosemary sprigs

4 fresh thyme sprigs

6 garlic cloves

2 tablespoons red wine
vinegar, plus more
for serving

Six ½-inch slices
sourdough bread

1 cup fresh flat-leaf parsley,
roughly chopped

Call it British, call it Tuscan, call it one strata of a Mexican torta. Who knows? Toasted bread and properly cooked beans is a killer. One of our initial cooks, a heavily tattooed (on the neck even) and fancy restaurant–trained gentleman named Jeff, put this recipe together. Cook the beans in the oven, low and slow, covered, with a little olive oil, lots of unsalted water, and some of the woodier herbs (rosemary, thyme) and you will create something very special. A heavy hand with salt when you assemble the final dish will jolt everything to life.

If using gigante beans, soak the beans in a large amount of water overnight. If these are fresh shell beans or smaller dried beans, there's no need to soak.

Preheat the oven to 300°F.

Drain the beans and put them in an oven-safe pot with a lid, something like a Dutch oven. Add enough water to just cover the beans and top with the olive oil. Add the rosemary, thyme, and garlic to the pot, apply the lid, and put into the oven. Depending on the type and size of the bean, the cooking time will vary. Check after 90 minutes (this is true for all beans, both fresh and dry—big and small). If needed, add more water to the pot to keep the beans submerged. For big beans, you can check every hour or so for 2 hours, but for smaller beans and fresh shell beans, start checking them every 30 minutes. When the beans are tender (taste them), they are done. Remove the pot from the oven. Now is a good time to season the beans with salt and pepper. Take 2 cups of beans from the pot and put them into a medium bowl. Reserve the rest. Add the red wine vinegar and a splash of olive oil to these beans and mush/smash, using the back of a spoon, into a rough puree.

When you are ready to eat, drizzle the bread with a little olive oil and toast in a skillet or a toaster until totally golden brown—do not underestimate or rush this step. Put the reserved cooked beans into a large bowl. Add the bean puree and most of the parsley and stir to combine. Tear the warm toasted bread into bite-size chunks and drop into the bowl of beans. Stir and convince the bread to absorb some of the liquid. Season with salt and pepper and a little more red wine vinegar if needed. Scatter the rest of the parsley on top and serve hot.

BEER BATTER MARKET PANCAKES

MAKES 4 TO 6 PANCAKES

2 cups all-purpose flour

2 teaspoons baking powder

2 teaspoons kosher salt

1 tablespoon cane sugar

One 16-ounce can Budweiser

2 tablespoons extra
  virgin olive oil

2 tablespoons grapeseed oil

3 scallions, cut into
  ¼-inch pieces

1 pound green beans or wax
  beans, cut in half

One 1-inch knob fresh
  ginger, peeled

½ cup pickled hot peppers,
  chopped small

¼ cup fresh flat-leaf parsley,
  finely chopped

½ cup unsweetened coconut
  flakes, toasted

Lemony mayo (optional)

While it appears on first glance to be a traditional breakfast pancake, this is very much a delivery system for random aging and spotty vegetable bits and offcuts hanging out in the back of the fridge; it's stuff not quite pretty enough to be a star, but still packed with good flavor, and like everyone, we just hate throwing away the ugly, unpretty scraps and knobs. The base recipe is vegan and utilizes beer to raise the batter. In our trials we first tried all the tonier beers from Tompkins Finest Deli around the corner on Avenue A, before agreeing that Budweiser was the perfect leavener. There are two versions here: one has a scallion pancake vibe and works with summer vegetables, and the second is ragingly full-on autumnal and shares DNA with the classic pasta *tortelli di zucca* (squash, sage, almond cookies).

For the pancakes, whisk together the flour, baking powder, salt, and sugar in a medium bowl. Add the whole can of beer and whisk until just combined. Stir in the olive oil. Add a little water (a couple tablespoons) to make it the consistency of thin pancake batter.

Add a tablespoon or so of the grapeseed oil to a large skillet over medium-high heat. Let the oil get very hot but not smoking and add the scallions. Cook until they start to brown and soften, a couple of minutes. Add the green beans to the skillet and cook over high heat, stirring every few minutes, until the beans are seared on at least one side and slightly softened. Transfer the bean mixture to a large mixing bowl. Using a Microplane, grate the ginger over the hot beans. Add the chopped hot peppers and parsley and season with salt and black pepper.

Heat a large nonstick skillet or griddle over medium heat. For each pancake, add a very thin layer of oil and drop a small handful of the green bean mixture into the center of the pan. Spread out the beans with the back of a spatula so there are little gaps in the green beans. Slowly add the batter over the beans—add just enough to cover and hold the beans together. Sprinkle the coconut on top of the raw batter. When the pancake starts to look dry around the edges, flip carefully and cook for a while longer on the other side. Serve this immediately with a lemony mayo or just as it is. It cuts nicely into wedges for sharing. You can also cook this pancake without the savory filling and eat it with maple syrup. The batter will last for 2 days in the refrigerator.

ZUCCA PANCAKE

3 scallions, cut into ¼-
inch pieces

1 butternut squash, chopped
and roasted

One 1-inch knob fresh
ginger, peeled

½ cup pickled hot peppers,
chopped small

¼ cup fresh flat-leaf parsley,
finely chopped

½ cup toasted vegan almond
cookie pieces

2 tablespoons shredded fresh
sage leaves

Follow the same method as above, but with these ingredients instead.
A sage-infused chickpea mayo (page 211) will top this off nicely.

LOADED WHITE SWEET POTATO

SERVES 6

TARRAGON GREEN SAUCE
1 shallot, minced
2 tablespoons red wine vinegar
1 tablespoon maple syrup
1½ cups chopped fresh tarragon
1 cup chopped fresh flat-
    leaf parsley
Zest of 2 lemons
2 serrano chiles, minced
½ cup capers packed in salt,
    rinsed and finely chopped
Extra virgin olive oil

Extra virgin olive oil
6 medium white sweet
    potatoes, scrubbed well

1 cup labne or sour cream, or
    vegan alternative
1 cup chopped dill pickles
Juice of 1 lemon

The problem with a lot of sweet potato preparations is that they fail to escape tasting like Thanksgiving. But white sweet potatoes are different. They roast into a yellow creaminess and are slightly less sugary than a yam or the orange version, and also not as starchy as the purple-skinned Japanese variety. Search for them in the fall. We get ours from a farm in New Jersey called Race Farm. The green sauce component here lassoes and tames the sweetness, and the chopped pickles finish the loaded quality with an appropriate vegetal crunch.

To make the tarragon green sauce, first soak the minced shallot in red wine vinegar and a splash of maple syrup for about 30 minutes. Mix together the tarragon, parsley, lemon zest, chiles, capers, and marinated shallot in a bowl. Add enough olive oil to make it saucelike. Season with salt and black pepper and red wine vinegar, if needed. The flavors will come together more on the day after the sauce is made.

Preheat the oven to 325°F. Lightly grease or line a baking sheet with parchment paper.

Rub the sweet potatoes with a little bit of olive oil, sprinkle the outside with salt, and place on the baking sheet. Bake until the potatoes, when prodded, yield completely—they should be totally tender all the way through—about 1 hour. Remove from the oven and let cool until they can be handled somewhat comfortably. Using a small paring knife, cut a slit in the top side of each potato. Gently open each slit, revealing the white inner flesh. Sprinkle a bit of salt and drop a couple tablespoons of tarragon green sauce into the openings and, using a fork, gently mash the flesh of the potato with the sauce to incorporate the two together. Add a dollop or two of labne, a spoonful of the chopped pickles, a squeeze of lemon, and some freshly ground black pepper to finish.

ROASTED ORANGE SWEET POTATO WITH OLIVE-RAISIN CHUTNEY

SERVES 6

OLIVE-RAISIN CHUTNEY
¾ cup Castelvetrano olives, pitted and chopped
¾ cup Pickled Golden Raisins (page 205), chopped
Zest and juice of 2 oranges
½ cup chopped fresh flat-leaf parsley

6 medium orange sweet potatoes, scrubbed well
¼ cup extra virgin olive oil, plus more for cooking
1 medium yellow onion, thinly sliced into half-moons
6 fresh sage leaves, finely chopped
3 scallions, thinly sliced
1 celery stalk, finely chopped

If the previous sweet potato dish can be seen as a wholly original breakout sensation, this one is *that* dish's slightly dull, kind of homely sibling. But it's a nice one to try if you find yourself flush with a crisper full of sage leaves and a cupboard full of the more lumpen, less flamboyant orange sweet potato variety.

For the olive-raisin chutney, mix together the olives, raisins, orange zest, orange juice, and parsley in a bowl. Add some of the raisin pickling liquid if the mixture seems a little dry. Set aside until ready to use or refrigerate for up to 3 days if using another day.

Preheat the oven to 325°F. Lightly grease or line a baking sheet with parchment paper.

Rub the washed potatoes with a little bit of olive oil and sprinkle the outside with salt. Place the potatoes on the baking sheet. Bake until the potatoes are very, very tender when pierced with a paring knife, about 1 hour. Remove from the oven and let cool a little until they can be handled.

While the potatoes are in the oven, prepare the sage-melted onion. Combine the olive oil, onion slices, and sage in a small saucepan. Over medium-low to low heat, cook the onions, stirring once in a while, until translucent, about 30 minutes. You don't want to brown them—they should be meltingly tender. Remove the pan from the heat and season the onions and oil with a medium pinch of salt and the same of pepper.

When the potatoes are cool enough to touch, cut a slit in the top side of the potatoes and open to reveal the orange inner flesh. Spoon a little bit of the melted onions and some of the onions' oil into the opening; using a fork, gently mash into the flesh. You can taste the potato at this point to see if it needs more salt. Spoon about a tablespoon or so of the chutney over the flesh (about 1 cup total), making sure it runs the length of the potato. Sprinkle with the scallions and celery.

SALT-AND-VINEGAR STRING BEANS

SERVES 6

1½ pounds fresh beans
(such as green or yellow
Romanos, wax beans, or
green beans), trimmed

Grapeseed oil

3 tablespoons malt vinegar

4 tablespoons malt vinegar
powder, plus more
for dusting

3 tablespoons extra
virgin olive oil

Flaky sea salt

Amazon.com is a bummer. We can all agree on this. They have made a career flattening the little, mighty, important mom and pop bookstores out of business. In New York city alone: St. Mark's Bookshop, Oscar Wilde Bookshop, Murder Ink, for example, all vanished. You can buy anything on Amazon. Compact discs, slacks, fetish hot sauces, you name it, they will sell it to you. We want this warm salad to taste as gripping and succulent as a paper cone of boardwalk fries minus the airborne fryer oil and fingered tubers. The key is powdered malt vinegar, which can be difficult to source. Amazon has it. But order it from a tiny online spice emporium instead; you might not get it in forty-eight hours, but we will all feel better about this commercial exchange.

Bring a heavily salted pot of water to a boil. Set up an ice bath. Gently drop the beans into the water and let boil for only 20 seconds or so. Immediately plunge them into the ice bath. Once they are cool, drain the beans well and dry with a clean kitchen towel.

In a large skillet, bring a little bit of grapeseed oil to almost smoking over high heat. Drop the beans into the skillet and move them around continuously so they get a nice sear on both sides. Transfer the beans into a large mixing bowl. Add the malt vinegar, malt vinegar powder, olive oil, and a lot of salt and pepper. The seasoning should remind you of boardwalk French fries. Top each serving with a sprinkle of flaky sea salt and a dusting of more malt vinegar powder. Eat with your fingers.

KELP AND VEGETABLE SCAMPI

SERVES 6

SCAMPI SAUCE

3 garlic cloves, very
    thinly sliced
1 cup dry white wine
Juice of 1 lemon
1 cup extra virgin olive oil
1½ teaspoons Korean
    chile flakes
2 tablespoons chopped fresh
    flat-leaf parsley

1 pound mixed vegetables
    (kabocha squash,
    Romanesco, string beans,
    and cauliflower work nicely),
    cut into 1½-inch pieces
Extra virgin olive oil
8 ounces fresh kelp
    (we source ours from
    Thimble Island Ocean
    Farm), cut down into
    noodlelike ribbons
½ cup chopped fresh flat-
    leaf parsley
1 cup coarse bread
    crumbs, toasted

Linguistically, authentically, and culinarily, this one is a minefield of inaccuracy. When it's available, we get our kelp fresh from Thimble Island Ocean Farms in Connecticut. Brent, who runs the place, is a seaweed advocate the likes of which we have rarely seen. Cool guy, great product. The scampi sauce is our attempt to mimic the intoxicating whiff of red-checkered-tablecloth seafood without yanking any fish, shelled or otherwise, from the roiled sea.

To make the scampi sauce, sauté the garlic in a bit of olive oil in a large skillet over low heat. Don't brown the garlic; just get it meltingly soft. Add the white wine and let the alcohol cook off. Take the pan off the heat. Whisk in the lemon juice and slowly whisk in the olive oil. Season with salt, pepper, the chile flakes, and parsley.

Preheat the oven to 400°F.

Lightly toss the vegetables with some olive oil, salt, and pepper and roast in the oven until browned and tender. This can be done ahead of time. Leftover roasted vegetables work well in this dish. Heat a table-spoon or so of olive oil in a large skillet over medium heat. Add the kelp to the pan, and stir to help it get evenly heated through. Add the roasted vegetables and stir to combine with the kelp. Add 1½ cups of the scampi sauce to the pan and toss thoroughly with everything else to coat the kelp and the vegetables. They should be glossy. Transfer to a large serving dish or individual bowls. Serve very hot with the chopped parsley and bread crumbs scattered over the top.

BBQ BAKED GIGANTE BEANS WITH POLENTA AND COLESLAW

SERVES 8

1 pound dried gigante beans, soaked overnight

Grapeseed oil

1 medium yellow onion, finely chopped

4 garlic cloves, minced

8 cups water

2 tablespoons espresso (we use Café Bustelo)

½ cup pureed tomatoes

¼ cup firmly packed dark brown sugar

4 teaspoons Gulden's brown mustard

2 tablespoons molasses

2 tablespoons Frank's RedHot sauce

¼ cup extra virgin olive oil

2 cups shredded green cabbage

2 tablespoons chopped fresh dill

½ cup Chickpea Mayo (page 211)

Juice of 1 lemon

Grapeseed oil

8 Polenta Planks (see page 207)

Speaking of gut-level, primal foodstuffs, is there anything more satisfying than an overloaded platter of regional American barbecue? Something greasy, stringy, sweet, and gristle-laden? But what about the hopeless descent into gastrointestinal shame that follows up the hillock of saturated translucent paper plates? Is there another way? Could this actually be pulled off without slow-cooked bovine or swine, or vegetarianly speaking, no vital wheat gluten as an analogue?

Preheat the oven to 300°F.

Drain the beans and put in a sturdy oven-safe pot, like a Dutch oven. In a medium pot over medium-high heat, add enough grapeseed oil to coat the bottom. Add the onion and cook until soft and translucent, about 12 minutes. Add the garlic and cook until not raw anymore, basically. Add the water, espresso powder, tomato puree, brown sugar, mustard, molasses, and hot sauce and bring to a rolling boil. Remove the pot from the heat and pour the liquid over the beans. Add the olive oil to the beans and juice. Cover tightly with aluminum foil or a lid and put in the oven. This is going to take a while. Check after 2 hours and make sure not too much of the liquid has evaporated. If it has, just add more water, cover, and cook some more. Check every hour or so until the beans are tender. Remove from the oven and season generously with salt and pepper. Let sit—the beans will absorb a lot of this liquid and release starch to make a thick sauce.

Mix together the cabbage with the dill, mayo, lemon juice, and some salt and pepper in a medium bowl. In a large nonstick or cast-iron skillet set over medium heat, heat a few tablespoons of grapeseed oil until shimmering. For each serving, sear a polenta plank on one side until golden brown and a little crispy, then flip it and sear the other side. Transfer to a plate, top generously with beans and bean sauce, and finish with a mound of the cabbage slaw.

BBQ CARROTS WITH CASHEW CREAM AND CORN CHIPS

SERVES 6

12 large carrots, cut into
  irregular 1½-inch pieces

Extra virgin olive oil

1½ cups BBQ sauce (page
  134), pureed and simmered
  for 10 minutes

½ cup Cashew Cream
  (page 205)

1 cup crushed corn chips (we
  like Have'a corn chips)

2 cups pea shoots or baby
  mustard greens (arugula
  would work in a pinch)

Juice of 1 lemon

We love carrots. But we've never had an amazing, life-changing carrot. However, that does not diminish any of our desires to wax rhapsodic about the orange root with the actually-not-that-delicious green top. Here we roast them deeply and then drench in barbecue sauce. The cashew cream keeps the acidity in check, and the re-toasted corn chips dial down the angelic quality. You can really sink your teeth into this number.

Preheat the oven to 400°F. Line a baking sheet with parchment paper.

Toss the carrots in a bowl with a few tablespoons of olive oil, a big pinch of salt, and some pepper. Transfer to the baking sheet and spread into a single layer. Roast in the oven until they are almost done, 15 to 20 minutes. Remove the pan from the oven, raise the oven temperature to 475°F, and drizzle 1 cup of the BBQ sauce over the carrots. Use a spoon to toss the carrots in the sauce so they are well coated. Return the pan to the oven and let cook until they are caramelized, sticky, and tender, 5 to 7 minutes more. Remove from the oven and let cool briefly.

To serve, create a low mound of carrots on a large plate. You can drizzle the extra ½ cup BBQ sauce over them if you'd like. Drizzle the cashew cream (in maybe a fancy zigzagged pattern; however, any design will do) all over the carrots. Scatter the crushed chips over the carrot mound, then top with some greens (pea shoots or something similar) that have been tossed in a little lemon juice and salt. Serve hot while the chips are still crisp and the greens still have their integrity.

CONFIT POTATOES

Upon completion of this recipe you will be left with a bumper crop of spent oil. You will pour it into a container once it has cooled, and leave it on the counter for many weeks. You will use straight from the bottle fresh oil for all of your other cooking, and the cling film–wrapped container will begin to collect dust near the spoon trivet. This oil tastes only faintly of potato and is fine to use for almost any other savory and sweet application. Use it up.

There are two versions below: Oreganato, which mimics a Long Island City old-school Italian American baked clam, and "New Bay," which makes us oddly homesick for Baltimore, Maryland.

"NEW BAY" POTATOES

SERVES 6

Grapeseed oil

2 pounds Confit Potatoes (page 210; 2 tablespoons Old Bay seasoning added to the oil while cooking and salt reduced to 1 tablespoon)

Zest and juice of 2 lemons

2 teaspoons Old Bay seasoning

4 scallions, thinly sliced

2 cups crushed potato chips (preferably kettle cooked, very crunchy)

Heat a large skillet over medium-high heat. Add just a small splash of grapeseed oil and the potatoes (this may need to be done to two batches so as to not crowd the pan). Sear the potatoes, flipping with a spatula as needed, until crispy and browned on both sides. Transfer the hot potatoes to a large bowl. Toss with the lemon zest, lemon juice, Old Bay seasoning, and some pepper. Serve right away topped with a scattering of the scallions and a small handful of the crushed potato chips.

POTATOES OREGANATO

SERVES 6

Grapeseed oil

2 pounds Confit Potatoes
(page 210; with 4 garlic
cloves and 2 fresh rosemary
sprigs added to the oil
while cooking)

Zest and juice of 2 lemons

2 tablespoons white wine
syrup reduced by half

1 cup finely ground plain
(unseasoned) bread crumbs

2 teaspoons dried oregano

1 teaspoon crushed red
pepper flakes

½ cup fresh flat-leaf parsley,
roughly chopped

Heat a large skillet over medium-high heat. Add just a tiny bit of grapeseed oil to the pan, then add the potatoes (in two batches, if necessary). Sear the potatoes, flipping with a spatula as needed, until crispy and browned on both sides. Transfer the hot potatoes to a large bowl. Toss the potatoes with the lemon zest, lemon juice, and reduced white wine syrup. Add a generous amount of salt and black pepper to the potatoes. In a small bowl, mix together the bread crumbs, oregano, and red pepper flakes. Sprinkle the seasoned bread crumbs, a few tablespoons at a time, over the hot potatoes. Gently toss the potatoes with the crumbs. Continue to add bread crumbs until the potatoes are coated in a thin layer, not clumpy but also not bare in any spots. Eat right away with some chopped parsley on top.

BRAISED COLLARD GREENS WITH HOT SAUCE AND HONEY

SERVES 6

Extra virgin olive oil

2 medium yellow onions, cut into small dice

4 garlic cloves, sliced paper thin

2 tablespoons tomato paste

¼ cup cider vinegar

1 tablespoon raw sugar

½ cup water

1 large bunch collard greens, stemmed and sliced into 1-inch strips

½ cup hot sauce (we like Frank's RedHot for this)

2 tablespoons honey or maple syrup (for the vegan version)

Korean chile flakes (optional)

Seared Polenta Planks (see page 207; optional)

Toasted sesame breadsticks

Collard greens seem to get no respect unless they have a ham hock or other pork-related seasoning buoy bobbing away in their Dutch oven. We strongly disagree with this. We are year-long champions of collard greens, and recognize both their humility and long-cooked chew as belonging to one of our favorite greens. If you are vegan and opposed to honey, maple syrup can slide right in without rumpling anyone's ethical stance.

Heat a couple tablespoons of olive oil in a deep pot over medium heat. Add the onions and a good pinch of salt and cook until the onions are totally soft and begin to take on some color, about 15 minutes. Add the garlic and cook for a few minutes more, until it just begins to become translucent. Add the tomato paste and raise the heat a little. Cook out the tomato paste until it turns into a deeper, more brown than red, color. Add the cider vinegar and raw sugar and scrape the bottom of the pot with some vigor to get any of the tomato paste and onions that may be stuck. Add the water and reduce the heat to medium-low. Add all the collard greens to the pot and cover with a lid. Let this go for a little while.

It's a good time to mix up the sauce. In a small bowl, combine the hot sauce and honey (or maple syrup for vegan) until it is one homogeneous liquid. If you want it a bit more spicy, add some chile flakes.

Check the collards after 15 minutes and, using a spoon, stir so that the leaves on the bottom come to the top and everything gets cooked evenly. Replace the lid and cook for about another 15 minutes more. Once the greens are tender and have become a dark forest-green color they are done. Remove from the heat and season with salt and pepper. To serve, heap into a bowl, either on top of a plank of seared polenta or not, and drizzle with the sauce and top with toasted sesame breadsticks.

GRIDDLED YUBA WITH SNAP PEAS, RHUBARB, AND MINT

SERVES 6

2 rhubarb stalks, cut into
¼-inch slices

1 tablespoon cane sugar

2 tablespoons grapeseed oil

¼ cup ramps or scallions, cut
into ¼-inch pieces

2 cups Marinated Yuba Strips
(page 210)

1 cup snap peas or snow
peas, blanched

4 tablespoons seasoned rice
wine vinegar

1 teaspoon crushed red
pepper flakes

1 bunch fresh mint

Nice olive oil (optional)

Scapece is an Italian-in-origin dish, and it is fantastic—usually utilizing shallow-oil-fried zucchini until it is fully engorged, along with some sort of allium element and a blanket of fresh mint. There are variations, of course. This is our clunky springtime version. Do it when the snap peas are plopped down right next to the rhubarb stalks in adjacent crates at the greenmarket. Yuba is around for slang and chew, but you can omit it, if you like.

In a small bowl, toss the cut rhubarb with the sugar and a small pinch of salt. Let sit for at least 30 minutes; the sugar-salt combination will slightly cure the rhubarb.

In a large skillet, heat the grapeseed oil over medium-high heat until shimmering. Add the ramps and cook until they just begin to brown and soften. Add the yuba next and cook, stirring frequently, so the yuba ribbons separate and begin to brown and caramelize. Add the snap peas last and cook for just a minute more until they are heated through. Transfer everything from the skillet into a large bowl. Add the rhubarb, rice wine vinegar, red pepper flakes, and salt and black pepper. If it seems dry at all, add a small splash of nice olive oil. Tear in a generous amount of fresh mint, toss one last time to combine, and it's ready to eat.

TAHINI-ROASTED CAULIFLOWER WITH TANGERINES AND HAZELNUTS

SERVES 6

½ cup tahini

¼ cup extra virgin olive oil

1 tablespoon maple syrup

2 teaspoons kosher salt

1 teaspoon freshly ground
   black pepper

1 large head cauliflower, cut
   into 1-inch slabs

½ cup sesame seeds, toasted

4 tangerines, zested,
   peeled, and separated
   into segments

1 Fresno chile, seeded and
   finely chopped

½ cup fresh cilantro, chopped

1 cup hazelnuts, toasted
   and crushed

Juice of 1 lemon

Consider this one a cautionary tale. Tahini allowed to breach oven doors and experience dry, hot heat does strange things. It Kentucky fries itself. It crisps and growls and cakes whatever it is cloaking in a nonoily sesame shroud. But don't stop reading just yet. The addition of tangerine suprêmes will take control and vein this salad with Tang-like comeuppance. Crunchy hazelnuts are lurking around, hidden underneath the cruciferous parts, thankful to have not been asked to gianduia themselves into forced obsolescence.

Preheat the oven to 475°F. Lightly grease a baking sheet.

Mix together the tahini, olive oil, maple syrup, salt, and black pepper in a shallow bowl. Gently dip the cauliflower slabs, one at a time, into the tahini mixture, using your hands to thoroughly coat each piece. Place each slab on the baking sheet and roast in the oven until the cauliflower is browned and just tender, 15 minutes. Remove from the oven and immediately sprinkle with the toasted sesame seeds. Set aside.

In a small bowl, mix together the tangerine zest, chile, cilantro, hazelnuts, and lemon juice. To serve, place a piece or a few pieces of cauliflower on a plate, gently tear tangerine segments in half and scatter on top of the cauliflower, and sprinkle the zest-chile-cilantro-nut mixture over everything.

GARLIC-BRAISED ESCAROLE WITH APPLES AND THYME

SERVES 6

Extra virgin olive oil

2 medium yellow onions, finely chopped

4 garlic cloves, sliced paper thin

2 tablespoons cider vinegar

½ cup water

3 heads escarole, cut into 1-inch pieces

4 fresh thyme sprigs, leaves picked

2 sweet and tart apples, sliced ¼-inch thick

½ cup Hammered Mushrooms (page 207), finely chopped

½ cup chopped fresh flat-leaf parsley

Young market escarole is fantastic raw, the hearts that are pale greenish-white. But if you desire a succulent, chewy, and slippery alternative, stove-top-braise some in a big pot with a garlicky base of olive oil. Add the apples and preexisting mushrooms right before serving. There's no actual crunchiness, but plenty of stick-to-your-ribs textural reward here.

Heat a few tablespoons of olive oil in a large deep pot over medium-high heat and add the onions and a large pinch of salt. Cook, stirring occasionally, until browned and tender, about 15 minutes. Add the garlic and cook for just a minute more. Stir in the cider vinegar, being sure to scrape the bottom of the pot well. Let the vinegar cook down for about a minute, then add the water and all the escarole. Reduce the heat to low and cover the pot. Cook, checking and stirring every 10 minutes or so, until all the escarole has just wilted. Taste for salt and add pepper and the thyme leaves. When ready to eat, drain off any excess liquid from the warm escarole and toss it with the apples and mushrooms. Finish with the parsley on top.

FRIED RICE AND BEANS

SERVES 4 TO 6

1 tablespoon hot chile sauce

1 tablespoon seasoned rice wine vinegar

2 tablespoons tamari

1 tablespoon extra virgin olive oil

4 star anise

2 cups jasmine rice

1 scallion, shredded

2 cups cooked black-eyed peas, rice beans, or other quick-cooking small bean

Extra virgin olive oil

Seasoned rice wine vinegar

1 teaspoon Korean chile flakes

½ cup Spicy Mayo (page 212)

2 cups smashed cucumbers (see page 72)

½ cup fresh mint

½ cup fresh Thai basil

½ cup fresh cilantro

Cooking jasmine rice with a few star anise pods and some other bonus seasoning will turn this floral-yet-tame grain exciting. We realized after cooking rice like this a few times it had an almost pho-like flavor profile. We had some beans quarted up in the fridge, so we sent our facilities manager to the August greenmarket to grab Thai basil, mint, and cilantro. We smashed up some chilled cucumbers for a temperature contrast. We mixed it all together and voilá. This one is great the next day, straight out of the Tupperware, for lunch.

To cook the rice, bring 3½ cups water to a boil in a large pot. Add the chile sauce, rice wine vinegar, tamari, olive oil, and star anise. Rinse the jasmine rice in a colander until the water runs clear. Add to the boiling seasoned water. Bring back to a boil and then drop to a simmer, cover, and cook for exactly 8 minutes (set a timer). Remove from the heat (keep the lid on) and let the residual heat carry over and complete the cooking for 15 minutes (set a timer). Spread out the warm rice on a baking sheet to cool. Pick out all the star anise pods.

To serve, griddle the scallions with a little olive oil in a sauté pan until slightly charred, about 6 minutes. Add the beans and part of the cooled rice to create a proper proportion of beans to rice. Cook, flipping around, until the rice gets warmed and speckled with brown flecks. Scrape into a mixing bowl and season to taste with salt, pepper, olive oil, rice wine vinegar, and chile flakes. Portion into bowls and top with the spicy mayo, smashed cucumbers, and equal parts of all of the herbs. Serve immediately.

Soups
and Stews

RUSSET POTATO–COCONUT SOUP

SERVES 4

POTATO SKINS
6 russet potatoes
Extra virgin olive oil
Korean chile flakes

2 tablespoons extra
    virgin olive oil
2 medium yellow onions, cut
    into small dice
4 garlic cloves, minced
One 4-inch piece fresh ginger,
    peeled and minced
6 large russet potatoes,
    peeled and cut into
    1-inch pieces
1½ cups full-fat coconut milk
2 tablespoons maple syrup
Hot chile oil (page 205)
Lemon
Fresh cilantro, chopped
Scallion, chopped

We run this soup almost every day from early November until it gets too balmy for broths and stews in the spring. Use a starchy russet potato, nothing too fancy or waxy. A food mill is key for the texture on this. And no, we don't know why this uni-tasking tool is so expensive, either. A blender will turn this from magical into a gluey mess. Keep your potato skins extra crisp and hand-crush them right on top before serving, their presence an amplitude of tubery spudness.

Preheat the oven to 400°F.

For the potato skins, bake the potatoes until they can easily be pierced with a fork, about 1 hour. Scoop out the flesh and reserve for another use. Massage the skins with olive oil and season with salt, pepper, and chile flakes. Bake the skins until crisped, 8 to 15 minutes.

In a big soup pot over medium-high heat, heat the olive oil until shimmering. Add the onions and a big pinch of salt. Cook, stirring frequently, until the onions are soft and begin to take on color, about 10 minutes. If the bottom of the pot gets too dark, add some water and scrape up the brown stuff. Add the garlic and ginger and cook until aromatic and they start to soften, 3 to 4 minutes. Add the potatoes to the pot and add enough water to cover the potatoes. Bring to a boil. Lower the heat and cook until the potatoes are fall-apart done. Add the coconut milk and maple syrup and season aggressively with salt and pepper. Pass everything through a food mill (or use an immersion blender just a little bit) but not a blender (will turn the mixture gluey). Serve really hot with chile oil, a squeeze of lemon, cilantro, scallions, and the crunchy potato skins.

ROASTED CAULIFLOWER SOUP

SERVES 4

2 heads cauliflower,
roughly chopped

Extra virgin olive oil

2 medium yellow onions, cut
into small dice

2 celery stalks, cut into
small dice

2 garlic cloves, minced

Rhubarb Mostarda
(recipe follows)

Cauliflower soup is cauliflower soup. It's nothing terribly exciting, but it makes for a terrific base to showcase something cool and weird that can't be served in a huge portion. And besides, why does everything have to be the greatest thing you have ever eaten in your life? Relax. The rhubarb mostarda garnish is the real headliner. We like to use brown mustard seeds to highlight the pink and brown-ness of the chutney. Warm up your pureed soup and spoon the cold rhubarb mix right on top. Eat quickly for the dual temperature rush.

Preheat the oven to 450°F.

Toss the cauliflower with olive oil, salt, and pepper. Distribute the cauliflower over two baking sheets so the cauliflower is in a single layer and the pieces have a little space between them. Roast in the oven until well browned, 15 to 20 minutes.

Meanwhile, heat olive oil in a sturdy soup pot over medium-high heat. Add the onions and celery and a big pinch of salt and cook until the onions start to brown and the celery softens, 15 to 20 minutes. Add some water if things are getting too brown. Lower the heat and add the garlic. Cook until the garlic softens a bit. Add the roasted cauliflower to the pot and enough water or broth to just cover. Bring to a boil and let cook for about 15 minutes, just so the flavors will come together. Season with salt and pepper and puree in a blender or with an immersion blender until very, very smooth. Serve with a dollop of rhubarb mostarda. This soup is a good way to use up leftover roasted cauliflower you may have in your refrigerator.

RHUBARB MOSTARDA

MAKES ABOUT 2 CUPS

1 pound rhubarb, cut into
   ¼-inch pieces
½ cup golden raisins,
   roughly chopped
¼ cup raw sugar
1 tablespoon brown
   mustard seeds
1 teaspoon Dijon mustard
½ teaspoon dry mustard
¼ cup sherry vinegar
¼ cup water
1½ teaspoons kosher salt

Combine half of the rhubarb, the raisins, sugar, mustard seeds, Dijon mustard, dry mustard, sherry vinegar, and water in a medium saucepan. Bring to a boil over medium-high heat, then reduce to a simmer and let cook until the mixture becomes jammy and the rhubarb has broken down mostly, about 15 minutes. Take the pan off the heat and add the other half of the cut rhubarb. Let the chutney cool a little before using—it will thicken and the flavors will meld together.

WHITE SWEET POTATO AND LEEK SOUP

SERVES 4

Extra virgin olive oil

2 cups chopped leeks
(washed well)

2 garlic cloves, minced

2 pounds white sweet
potatoes, peeled and cut
into 1/2-inch cubes

1 cup full-fat coconut milk

Fresh lemon juice

Freshly grated nutmeg

One pot, just a few ingredients. Genetically related to vichyssoise but served hot, because cold potatoes of any color are good for nothing. We serve it with a wedge of Italian green onion pancake, which is basically a scallion pancake seasoned like Italian food.

Heat olive oil in a deep soup pot over medium heat until shimmering. Add the leeks and some salt and cook until totally, meltingly soft and take on a little color, about 20 minutes. Add the garlic and cook a bit more. Add the sweet potatoes to the pot and enough water to cover. Bring it all to a boil, then reduce to a simmer until the potatoes are falling apart. Add the coconut milk and season again with salt and pepper. Puree it all with a blender or immersion blender or food mill. Season with lemon juice and a few gratings of fresh nutmeg. Serve hot.

ITALIAN GREEN ONION PANCAKES

MAKES 4 PANCAKES

2 cups all-purpose flour

1 teaspoon kosher salt

1 cup boiling water

¼ cup plus 1 tablespoon extra
virgin olive oil

2 cups thinly sliced scallions

2 tablespoons fennel seeds,
toasted and crushed

1 tablespoon crushed red
pepper flakes

2 teaspoons dried oregano

1 teaspoon freshly ground
black pepper

¼ cup grapeseed oil

Put the flour and salt into the bowl of a food processor. With the food processor running, slowly add most of the water—about ¾ cup—and 1 tablespoon of the olive oil. Let the food processor run for about 15 seconds, and if the dough does not come together, add a little bit more water until it just does. Transfer the dough to a lightly floured surface and knead for a minute to make a smooth ball. Wrap in plastic wrap and let rest for 30 minutes at room temperature.

Mix together the fennel seeds, red pepper flakes, oregano, and black pepper in a small bowl. Divide the pancake dough into 4 pieces and roll each one into a smooth ball. Roll one ball out into a disk about 8 inches in diameter on a lightly floured surface. Spread a very thin layer of olive oil over the top of the disk either using your fingertips or a pastry brush. Roll the disk up like a jelly roll, then twist the roll into a tight spiral, tucking the end underneath. Flatten gently with the palm of your hand, then reroll into an 8-inch disk. These multiple twisting and rolling steps will create a flaky texture. Spread on another very thin layer of olive oil, sprinkle with a pinch of the fennel seed mixture, then sprinkle with ½ cup of the scallions. Roll it up like a jelly roll again. Twist into a spiral, flatten gently, and reroll into a 7-inch disk. Repeat this whole process with the remaining balls of dough.

Heat the grapeseed oil in a nonstick skillet over medium-high heat until shimmering. Very carefully slide a pancake into the hot oil and cook for 2 minutes—gently shaking the pan if needed—until the underside is golden brown. Using tongs, carefully flip the pancake and cook for another 2 minutes until the other side is golden brown. Place the pancake on a baking sheet lined with paper towels and sprinkle generously with salt. Repeat the frying process with the other pancakes. Slice each pancake into 4 wedges and serve immediately.

RED LENTIL STEW

SERVES 4

Extra virgin olive oil

2 medium yellow onions, finely chopped

2 celery stalks, finely chopped

1 carrot, finely chopped

2 tablespoons tomato paste

Red wine vinegar

6 garlic cloves, minced

3 fresh rosemary sprigs, leaves picked and finely chopped

1 bunch fresh thyme, leaves picked

2 cups red lentils, rinsed

6 cups water

Cooked brown rice (page 211)

Chopped fresh flat-leaf parsley

We have fond memories of hanging out at the many Ethiopian and Eritrean restaurants of Washington, DC, and scooping up *mesir wat/ tsebi mesir* (red lentil stew) with flaps of torn injera. This stew is our tribute to this killer dish but made with Mediterranean flavors since Superiority Burger is really just an Italian restaurant disguised as a tiny veggie burger joint. Nothing effete here though; the lentils get packed side by side along with brown rice and a fistful of hacked parsley. One twist of the spoon and the whole thing collapses into a stewy mess.

Heat some olive oil in a large soup pot over medium heat and add the onions, celery, carrot, and some salt. Cook until all the vegetables start to soften and take on a little color, about 20 minutes. Add the tomato paste and cook until it starts to brown. Deglaze with a splash of red wine vinegar. Add the garlic, rosemary, and thyme and cook until it becomes aromatic. Add the lentils and water and bring to a boil. Reduce the heat and let simmer until the lentils are fully cooked and the sauce thickens. Season with more salt and some pepper. Serve over a scoop of brown rice with chopped parsley and a splash of red wine vinegar.

CREAMY WILD RICE SOUP

1 cup unsalted ca-
shews, roasted

2 tablespoons extra
virgin olive oil

2 large Spanish onions, cut
into small dice

3 carrots, cut into small dice

3 celery stalks, cut into
small dice

4 garlic cloves, minced

½ cup all-purpose flour

½ cup dry white wine

12 cups vegetable
broth or water

1½ cups wild rice

3 fresh thyme sprigs,
leaves picked

Chopped fresh flat-
leaf parsley

Grilled bread

Before playing around with this soup, our wild rice (Canada rice?) experience was mostly vague remembrances of foil-wrapped Pyrex casseroles from 80s potlucks. Before you add the cashew cream and olive oil, this cooks into a murky gray brodo rife with blown-out husks of also gray wild rice. It's kind of like faux mushroom-barley soup, unnecessarily so, as it contains neither.

Soak the cashews overnight in plenty of water. Drain and blend in a high-powered blender. Gradually add water while the blender is running until the mixture has the consistency of heavy cream. This should give you about 2 cups of cashew cream.

Heat the olive oil in a deep soup pot over medium-high heat. Add the onions and a large pinch of salt and cook, stirring frequently, until the onions begin to brown and soften, about 10 minutes. Add the carrots, celery, and garlic to the pot, reduce the heat to medium-low, and cook on low heat until the vegetables are totally soft, about 20 minutes. Add the flour and cook, stirring constantly, for a couple minutes to ensure it loses its raw flavor. Add the white wine and let most of the alcohol cook off. Add the broth and rice to the pot and bring to a boil. Once the liquid is boiling, reduce the heat and let simmer until the rice is tender, about 25 minutes. Turn off the heat and add the thyme leaves. Add 1 to 2 cups of the cashew cream, depending on how creamy you want the soup to be. Season with more salt and some pepper. Serve topped with a little bit of chopped parsley and a piece of grilled bread on the side.

CREAM OF FAVA BEAN SOUP

SERVES 6

¼ cup extra virgin olive oil

2 medium yellow onions,
  finely chopped

2 celery stalks, finely chopped

4 garlic cloves, thinly sliced

2 cups raw cashews

2 tablespoons raw sugar

1 teaspoon crushed red
  pepper flakes

3 cups water

2 pounds frozen fava beans,
  thawed a little

1 tablespoon malt vinegar

2 scallions, thinly sliced

Fried Salt-and-Vinegar
  Wonton Wrappers (see page
  205; optional)

Frozen fava beans are fine to use for this soup. Fresh favas shouldn't get hammered like this—it would be a shame, after putting in all that time and effort hulling and peeling. Our favorite way to garnish this soup is with a squirt of malt vinegar, a few shredded scallions, and, time permitting, wonton skins that are shallow-fried until bubbly and then dusted with malt vinegar powder and plenty of salt.

Heat the olive oil in a large saucepan over medium-low heat. Add the onions, celery, and garlic and cook, stirring often and adding a splash or so of water if the bottom of the pan gets too brown, until golden brown, 30 to 40 minutes. Season with salt and black pepper. Add the cashews, sugar, red pepper flakes, and water and bring the mixture to a simmer. Cook until the vegetables are very soft and losing their structure, 10 to 15 minutes.

Blend one-third of the fava beans with one-third of the vegetable mixture in a blender, adding some cooking liquid from the vegetable mixture as needed to thin, until very smooth, about 2 minutes. Press the puree through a fine-mesh strainer into a medium saucepan; discard the solids. Working in two batches, repeat with the remaining favas and vegetable mixture, adding water as needed if you run out of cooking liquid. If the soup is still very thick, thin it with water until you get a velvety, pourable consistency. Stir the malt vinegar into the soup. Season with more salt and black pepper and warm over medium-low until heated through.

Serve immediately, topped with scallions and fried wontons, if you like.

CARROT SOUP WITH MINT AND PEANUTS

SERVES 6

2 pounds carrots, cut into
½-inch coins

1 jalapeño chile, cut into
½-inch rings

Grapeseed oil

2 medium yellow onions,
finely chopped

4 garlic cloves, thinly sliced

4 cups water

¼ cup white miso paste

2 cups carrot juice

½ cup fresh mint, roughly
chopped

2 cups pea shoots

Juice of ½ lemon

½ cup full-fat coconut milk

1 cup unsalted peanuts,
toasted and chopped

This soup tastes better at room temperature. Too hot and the flavor is muted, not as carrot-ful as it is at, say, 65 degrees. That's a difficult temperature to maintain, so we recommend making, garnishing, and eating it right away, washing all the dishes, turning out the lights, closing the kitchen for the day, all in one shot.

Preheat the oven to 425°F. Lightly grease a baking sheet.

Place half of the carrots in a medium bowl and toss with the jalapeño, 2 tablespoons grapeseed oil, and salt and black pepper. Transfer to the baking sheet and roast until the carrots are well browned and tender, about 20 minutes.

While the carrots are in the oven, heat a few more tablespoons oil in a large deep soup pot over medium-high heat. Add the onions and a pinch of salt. Let the onions cook, stirring frequently, until they start to brown and are fully translucent, 8 to 10 minutes. Add the garlic and cook for a minute more. Add the water to the pot along with the remaining carrots and bring to a boil over high heat. By now, the roasted carrots and jalapeño should be done. Add these to the pot as well. Cook until the raw carrots are tender, about 30 minutes. Stir in the miso paste. Puree the soup in batches in a blender—adding a little carrot juice each time—until it is velvety smooth. Transfer the soup back into the pot until ready to serve. If the soup seems too thick, add a little more carrot juice. When you are ready to eat, toss the mint, pea shoots, and lemon juice in a medium bowl to combine. Season with salt and black pepper. Ladle the soup into bowls and top with a small drizzle of the coconut milk, the chopped peanuts, and a mound of the pea shoot-mint salad. This soup actually tastes best not piping hot—we recommend eating it at ambient temperature.

TOMATO-STAINED BLACK-EYED PEA SOUP WITH ELBOWS

SERVES 6

2 tablespoons extra
virgin olive oil

2 Spanish onions, cut into
small dice

4 celery stalks, cut into
small dice

6 garlic cloves, sliced
paper thin

2 tablespoons tomato paste

¼ cup red wine vinegar

1 fresh rosemary sprig, leaves
picked and minced

One 28-ounce can crushed
tomatoes

3 cups dried black-eyed peas

1 to 2 tablespoons raw sugar

2 cups slightly undercooked
elbow macaroni

Fresh basil leaves

Crushed red pepper flakes
(optional)

The stakes were considerably high on this one as it involved us trying to rip off a classic Italian *cacciucco* without using any of the aquatic items that make that classic soup taste like it does. We originally served this with a handful of De Cecco ditalini pasta floating on top, but pulled the elbow macaroni switcheroo, because, let's be honest here, elbows are the queen of pasta.

Heat the olive oil in a large deep soup pot over medium heat. Add the onions and celery and a big pinch of salt and cook, stirring regularly, until totally soft and starting to take on some color, 10 to 12 minutes. Add the garlic and cook until the pieces become translucent, about 5 more minutes. Add the tomato paste—now stir more frequently—and cook until it goes from bright red to a more brick-red (red-brown) color, about 10 minutes. Add the red wine vinegar and use a spoon to scrape any of the stuck bits from the bottom of the pot. Add the rosemary, crushed tomatoes, black-eyed peas, and enough water to cover the peas by about 3 inches. Raise the heat and bring it all up to a boil. Reduce the heat to maintain a simmer and let it go until the peas are totally tender—this will take about an hour or so. The peas will release some starch that will thicken the broth a little—this is good! Check the seasoning for salt, black pepper, and sugar and adjust as needed. To serve, spoon the soup piping hot into a bowl and top with ¼ to ½ cup cooked elbow macaroni. Tear some basil leaves over the top of the pasta and add a pinch of red pepper flakes, if you like. Serve immediately, as the pasta will overcook in the hot broth.

PARSNIP AND FENNEL SOUP

SERVES 6

¼ cup honey or maple syrup
(for the vegan version)

1 teaspoon Korean chile flakes

½ teaspoon finely chopped
fresh thyme leaves

8 cups peeled and medium-
diced parsnips

Extra virgin olive oil

3 medium yellow onions,
finely chopped

2 cloves garlic, finely sliced
with a mandoline

½ cup dry white wine

2 teaspoons fresh thyme
leaves, finely chopped

3 fennel bulbs, tough outer
leaves removed, chopped

6 cups water

1 cup hazelnuts, toasted
and crushed

4 scallions, thinly sliced

We make things slightly more difficult by making you start a soup base on the stove while at the same time firing up the oven to roast the chunks of parsnip. The roasting adds a depth of flavor that cannot be captured simply by allowing the roots to simmer in a broth. Reserve some of the roasted parsnip pieces to float on top and the reinforcement of flavor will be complete. The fennel imparts a vegetal licorice flavor that will be tempered by the parsnips, and, yes, chafe the tuchus of all the licorice haters.

Combine the honey with the chile flakes and thyme in a bowl. Set aside.

Preheat the oven to 450°F. Lightly grease a baking sheet.

Toss the parsnips with a few teaspoons of olive oil and spread into a single layer on the baking sheet. Roast until the parsnips are well cara-melized and tender, about 25 minutes. Remove from the oven and set aside 1 cup of the cooked parsnips in a small bowl.

In a large deep soup pot, heat a few tablespoons of olive oil over medium-high heat. Add the onions along with a big pinch of salt and let them cook until they begin to brown and soften, about 12 minutes. Add the garlic and cook for a minute more, then add the white wine and let cook until the alcohol smell is gone, about 3 minutes. Add the chopped thyme, the rest of the sheet of roasted parsnips, the fennel, and water. Bring to a boil over high heat and then reduce to a simmer until the fen-nel is tender. Blend with an immersion blender in batches and transfer back into the soup pot. Check for seasoning and add salt and pepper as needed. When ready to serve, top each bowl of soup with a drizzle of the honey-thyme mixture, some of the reserved roasted parsnips, a sprinkle of the crushed hazelnuts, and the sliced scallions.

VEGETABLE SOUP WITH CURLY PARSLEY

SERVES 6

Extra virgin olive oil

3 medium yellow onions,
  finely chopped

2 carrots, cut into small dice

3 celery stalks, cut into
  small dice

2 red bell peppers, cut into
  small dice

4 garlic cloves, minced

2 tablespoons tomato paste

½ cup dry white wine

6 cups water

½ head green cabbage, cut
  into ¼-inch ribbons

Red wine vinegar (optional)

1 bunch greens (kale or Swiss
  chard), stems removed, torn
  into small pieces

Fresh curly parsley

White Italian bread, toasted,
  drizzled with extra virgin
  olive oil, rubbed with a
  garlic clove, and sprinkled
  with salt

The first time we made a batch of this we all stood around the back of the kitchen with decanted plastic pint containers and just slurped in silence. The layering of flavors and salting as you go, and the fried double-concentrated tomato paste, create about the most vibrant, exciting vegetable soup that we have ever had. Curly parsley is not essential, but deployed strategically around the rim and the visual red herring that this is just a boring old cup of broth gets throttled. Parsley has power.

Heat a slick of olive oil in a large deep soup pot over medium-high heat. Add the onions and a big pinch of salt and cook, stirring frequently, until the onions are starting to brown and are translucent, about 10 minutes. Add the carrots, celery, and bell peppers to the pot and cook for about 8 minutes more. Add the garlic and tomato paste. Cook for at least 5 more minutes, until the tomato paste starts to brown and stick to the bottom of the pot. Add the white wine and scrape up any stuck bits from the pot. Add the water and another large pinch of salt and bring to a boil. Reduce the heat, add the cabbage, and let simmer, just until the cabbage starts to get soft, about 10 minutes. Check the seasoning for salt and acidity (add a little red wine vinegar if the soup tastes flat) and black pepper. When ready to eat, add the greens to the very hot soup and let them wilt and turn a vibrant green color. Serve with a scattering of curly parsley, and a slice of the toasted bread.

Sweets

BREAD PUDDING

SERVES 10

10 slices old bread or buns

3½ cups full-fat coconut milk

1½ cups water

5 tablespoons cornstarch

3 tablespoons dark
  brown sugar

3 tablespoons raw sugar, plus
  more for sprinkling

1 tablespoon pure
  vanilla extract

1½ teaspoons kosher salt

Gelato (optional)

We've always been racked with guilt at the amount of bread we end up throwing away after using as many day-old rolls as possible for bread crumbs, croutons, thickening agents, you name it. Running a place that predominantly stuffs vegetables between bread means there's often a lot just hanging about. This was one of our first composed desserts, and tastes like Dutch pancakes once it has been given a quick sear in a hot skillet.

Preheat the oven to 350°F.

Cube the bread and toast in the oven until golden brown and mostly dried out. Put the bread cubes into a casserole dish. Whisk together the coconut milk, water, cornstarch, and sugars in a pot and put over medium-low heat. Let the mixture come to a low simmer and whisk frequently, until the custard thickens and can coat the back of a spoon, about 8 minutes. Add the vanilla and salt. Pour the custard over the bread cubes and let it soak for at least 20 minutes. Sprinkle with raw sugar. Bake for 25 to 35 minutes, until just set. Let cool for a little while and serve as is, or with a gelato topping.

CARROT CAKE

SERVES 12

Grapeseed oil

1½ cups cane sugar

1 cup extra virgin olive oil

1 cup vegan sour cream

1 tablespoon pure
   vanilla extract

2 cups all-purpose flour

1 teaspoon baking powder

1 teaspoon baking soda

1 teaspoon ground cinnamon

1 teaspoon kosher salt

2 cups grated carrots

This is the vegan version. To get some more lift, you can substitute four whole eggs for the vegan sour cream. We don't; we always stick with the vegan version, because an eggless baking challenge is very good for the brain.

Preheat the oven to 350°F. Grease a half sheet pan or jelly-roll pan with a little grapeseed oil and line the bottom with parchment paper.

Mix together the sugar, olive oil, sour cream, and vanilla in a large bowl. In another bowl, mix together all the dry ingredients. Add the dry to the wet ingredients and mix until mostly combined. Fold in the carrots but don't mix too much. Pour the batter into the prepared pan and spread evenly. Bake for about 20 minutes and check for doneness with a toothpick inserted into the center or a gentle press with your finger. Let cool on a wire rack for 15 minutes and serve.

BANANA BREAD

1 LOAF, SERVES 8

1 tablespoon olive oil for
   greasing the pan

1¼ cups all-purpose flour

1 teaspoon baking soda

1 teaspoon kosher salt

1 teaspoon ground cinnamon

1½ cups mashed very ripe
   bananas, plus 1 whole
   banana, roughly chopped

¾ cup cane sugar

½ cup regular or vegan
   sour cream

½ cup extra virgin olive oil

1 tablespoon pure
   vanilla extract

Turbinado sugar

Grapeseed oil for drizzling

Coconut Sorbet (page 198)

Chocolate–Olive Oil Sauce
   (recipe follows)

A crowd-pleaser of epic proportions. Baking a loaf of this will send the inhabitants of your house or apartment building into a frenzy of lust, as the odor of baking cinnamon, turbinado, and bananas permeates and breaches the walls. You want to use very ripe, nearly rotten bananas. We serve it with coconut sorbet and a heavy hand of chocolate-olive oil that sinks into the warm cake (it's really cake, not bread—we know no one is fooled) and magically shells itself into a chewy architecture on the frozen scoop.

Preheat the oven to 350°F. Lightly grease a 9-by-5-inch loaf pan.

Mix together the flour, baking soda, salt, and cinnamon in a large bowl. In another bowl, mix together the mashed banana, sugar, sour cream, olive oil, and vanilla. Pour the wet ingredients into the bowl with the flour mixture. Gently mix everything together—sprinkle in the chopped bananas while mixing and mix until just combined. Pour the batter into the loaf pan and sprinkle with a little turbinado sugar. Bake for 25 to 35 minutes, until a toothpick inserted into the center comes out clean or with some moist crumbs. Let cool a little before slicing. To serve, heat a small skillet over medium-high heat. Add a tiny bit of grapeseed oil. Griddle the bread on both sides until golden brown and warmed all the way through. Top with a scoop of coconut sorbet and drizzle with chocolate–olive oil sauce.

CHOCOLATE–OLIVE OIL SAUCE

MAKES ABOUT 1 CUP

8 ounces good dark chocolate

3 tablespoons extra
   virgin olive oil

Melt the chocolate in a bowl set over a pan of simmering water. Slowly stream in the olive oil while whisking constantly. Season aggressively with salt. Use immediately or, if it cools and hardens, just warm it up to bring it back to liquid.

CHOCOLATE CHIP–FREE CRUMBLE

MAKES ABOUT 4 CUPS

2 cups all-purpose flour

1 teaspoon baking powder

¾ teaspoon baking soda

1 teaspoon kosher salt

½ cup cane sugar

½ cup firmly packed dark
brown sugar

½ cup plus 1 tablespoon
grapeseed oil

¼ cup plus 1
tablespoon water

This one is lifted from our friends at the very excellent bakery Ovenly of Greenpoint, Brooklyn. This same recipe with chocolate chips is the greatest vegan chocolate chip cookie we have ever had. We omit the chocolate chips, spread the dough thin, and overbake it to get a crunchy crumble that pairs with gelato quite stunningly.

Whisk together the flour, baking powder, baking soda, and salt in a large bowl. In another bowl, combine the sugars and vigorously whisk in the grapeseed oil and water until incorporated. Cover or transfer to a sealable plastic bag and refrigerate overnight.

Preheat the oven to 350°F.

Divide the dough into 2 balls. Roll out each ball (on top of a sheet of parchment) to about ¼ inch thick and move the parchment to a baking sheet. Bake for 12 to 15 minutes, until cooked all the way—but not overcooked. Let cool completely on a wire rack, then crumble into irregular chunks for an ice cream crunch.

PEACH-BLUEBERRY BREADSTICK CRUMBLE

SERVES 8

6 cups blueberries and
  diced peaches

3 tablespoons instant tapioca

2 tablespoons (more or less)
  cane sugar

Fresh lemon juice or
  verjus as needed

2 cups sesame breadstick
  crumbs (ground in a food
  processor)

6 tablespoons dark
  brown sugar

2 teaspoons kosher salt

¾ cup extra virgin olive oil

2 tablespoons raw sugar

This one is very simple and the payoff is huge. A good Italian deli will have a serviceable sesame breadstick, either packaged or house made. Always put a larger baking sheet underneath to catch the eruptions of molten fruit magma. Any dribbles that leak to the bottom of the oven will burn and smell great for a few minutes before carbonizing and spewing smoke, turning your apartment or six-seat restaurant into an acrid no-fun zone.

Preheat the oven to 375°F.

Combine the cut fruit, tapioca, cane sugar (as needed), acidity in the form of lemon juice or verjus, and a pinch of salt in a large bowl. Let sit and macerate as you prepare the topping. In a medium bowl, mix together the breadstick crumbs, brown sugar, and salt. Pour in the olive oil and stir until the mixture resembles wet sand.

Transfer the fruit filling to a 9-inch square baking pan (or something comparable) and sprinkle generously with the breadstick topping. Sprinkle a little raw sugar on top of that (it will add a nice crunch to the topping) and bake for 40 minutes or so—until the top is well browned and the fruit filling looks gooey, jammy, and bubbling. Let it cool for at least 20 minutes before digging in. This also tastes really good straight out of the refrigerator—cold and congealed—like eating jam straight out of the jar.

SEARED POLENTA WITH MAPLED OLIVE OIL

SERVES 4

4 Polenta Planks
  (see page 207)
1 cup maple syrup
½ cup extra virgin olive oil
Gelato

The warm polenta slab here is the same one we use in savory applications. We blitz maple syrup and extra virgin olive oil together to make a sticky emulsified elixir that smacks of sweet melted butter. A smear of gelato on top and it's breakfast for dessert in the Sicilian quadrant of Montreal.

Warm the polenta slabs in a cast-iron skillet, getting a little color on each side. Mix the maple syrup and olive oil with an immersion blender until thick and emulsified, then season with salt. To serve, take a slab of polenta and drizzle it with the mapled olive oil. Top with gelato of your choosing.

NEUTRAL GELATO BASE

MAKES 2 LITERS

300 grams cane sugar

75 grams powdered milk

50 grams dextrose

1500 grams whole milk

500 grams heavy cream

When Superiority Burger first opened, we used eggs; eggs as a binder in the burger mix and eggs in our gelato bases. This proved to be a problem, as a good chunk of our customers (vegan or not) simply did not eat eggs. So we stopped using eggs entirely (and felt pretty good about it!) and also designed this eggless gelato base recipe with the assistance of Dana Cree, our pastry chef pal based out of Chicago. It took only four e-mails and a few 2 a.m. (her time) text messages and we knew we had a winner. This spins into a chewy and creamy base.

Mix together the dry ingredients in a bowl. In a large saucepan, heat the milk and heavy cream and whisk in the dry ingredients. Bring everything up to 180°F, whisking constantly so the milk solids do not scorch on the bottom of the pan. Hold the mixture at 180°F for 30 minutes to set the proteins. If you are doing an infusion, take these 30 minutes to infuse the base.

POPPY SEED: Infuse 2 cups poppy seeds during the 30-minute interval. Strain out half of the poppy seeds and blend with a few table-spoons of base liquid to create a paste. Add back into the base and strain everything through a fine-mesh strainer. Season with salt. Chill over-night and spin.

CARDAMOM–PUMPKIN SEED OIL: Infuse 2 cups gently toasted and crushed cardamom pods during the 30-minute interval. Grind with an immersion blender to break up the pods and strain through a fine-mesh strainer. Season with salt. Chill overnight. During the spinning process, drizzle ½ cup pumpkin seed oil into the machine midway through processing.

POLENTA: Cook polenta (page 207) but spread it very thin on a bak-ing sheet and then dry it out in the oven. Infuse the base with the dried polenta sheet during the 30-minute interval. Pulse gently with an immersion blender and strain through a fine-mesh strainer. Season with salt. Chill overnight and spin.

BLACK SESAME: Infuse 2 cups toasted black sesame seeds during the 30-minute interval. Strain out half of the sesame seeds and blend with a few tablespoons of base liquid to create a paste. Add back into base and strain everything through a fine-mesh strainer. Season with salt. Chill overnight and spin.

SORBET SYRUP

MAKES 4¼ CUPS

2 cups water

2 cups cane sugar

⅓ cup dextrose

This is a very thick syrup tool that will help you turn almost any fruit puree or juice into a luscious, delicate sorbet. Making sorbet is kind of a trip, because you are basically taking 100 percent fruit, and then sugaring it, and watering it way down, with the hopes that your finished product will taste like the most perfect version of the fruit you just diluted. That's strange to think about. It might not be total alchemy, but it's definitely science. We rely on malic acid, lime and lemon juice, to reincorporate any lost acidity. Texture is key in sorbets. Iciness is no good.

Bring the water to a boil. Add the dry ingredients. Return to a boil. Chill and reserve.

VARIATIONS

Fruit purees and juices vary wildly in sugar content. The following recipes may require tweaking as to the final amount of sorbet syrup you add. The base (pre-spinning) should taste slightly sweeter than you want (the freezing process will dull some of the sugar).

COCONUT SORBET

Mix together 2 cups sorbet syrup with 2 cups coconut milk and 2 cups coconut puree. Blend and season with fresh lime juice and salt. Spin.

CHOCOLATE SORBET

Blend 500 grams water with 400 grams sorbet syrup and 1 tablespoon cocoa powder and bring to a boil. Pour over 400 grams chopped chocolate and whisk to melt. Strain through a fine-mesh strainer and season with salt. Chill and spin.

GRAPEFRUIT SORBET

Peel the skin from about 10 grapefruit. Blanch the peels five times in boiling water to tame their bitterness. Simmer the peels in simple syrup until translucent. Combine equal parts grapefruit juice and chilled sorbet syrup. Using an immersion blender, blitz the peels into liquid. Season with malic acid and salt. Spin.

continues

DELI MELON SORBET

Combine equal parts melon juice (we get ours from a deli on Second Avenue, where it tastes fresh and melon-y year-round) and chilled sorbet syrup. Season with fresh lime juice, malic acid, and salt. Spin.

BLACKBERRY SORBET

Blend 2 pounds fresh blackberries into a thick puree. Combine equal parts puree and chilled sorbet syrup. Season with fresh lemon juice, malic acid, and salt. Spin.

STRAWBERRY SORBET

Hull and cut 2 pounds of strawberries and cover with a little cane sugar and fresh lemon juice overnight. The next day blend the macerated berries into a thick puree, keeping the seeds. Combine equal parts with chilled sorbet syrup. Season with fresh lemon juice, malic acid, and salt. Spin.

Pantry
Recipes

PUMP CHEESE

MAKES 3 CUPS

6 tablespoons grapeseed oil

1 medium yellow onion, thinly sliced

1 poblano pepper, chopped

1 jalapeño chile, thinly sliced

1 teaspoon ground cumin

1 tablespoon chile powder

2 teaspoons ground turmeric

1½ cups roasted cashews

1 russet potato, peeled and thinly sliced

1 large carrot, unpeeled and chopped

¼ cup nutritional yeast flakes

1 tablespoon hot pepper pickle juice or white wine vinegar

Heat the grapeseed oil in a medium saucepan over medium heat. Add the onion, poblano, and jalapeño and cook until well-caramelized and browned. Add the cumin, chile powder, and tumeric and cook for a few more minutes to release the oils from the spices. Add the cashews, potato, carrot, and about 4 cups of water to cover. Bring to a boil and simmer until everything is mushy. Stir in the nutritional yeast and pickle juice off the heat.

In batches, transfer the solid matter to a high-powered blender, adding some of the cooking liquid (or water) as necessary to create the desired cheeselike consistency. Season with salt and black pepper. You can add more tumeric if you want a more yellow hue, but be careful, as the tumeric flavor will begin to overpower everything.

PICKLED ONIONS AND OTHER ALLIUMS

MAKES 2 CUPS

2 cups golden balsamic vinegar

1 cup cane sugar

1 tablespoon Korean chile flakes

1 tablespoon kosher salt

2 medium red onions (or substitute ramps, garlic scapes, or shallots), thinly sliced

Bring the golden balsamic vinegar, sugar, chile flakes, and salt to rolling boil in a medium saucepan over high heat. Blanch the onions in the boiling vinegar for about 45 seconds. Remove from the pan and spread on a baking sheet to cool. Once they are cool, put the onions in a storage container. Let the pickling liquid cool also and pour over the onions to fully cover them. It's best to let the onions sit in this liquid overnight— they will turn translucent when they are ready.

FRIED SALT-AND-VINEGAR WONTON WRAPPERS

MAKES 8 FRIED WONTON WRAPPERS

1 quart grapeseed oil
8 square wonton wrappers
Malt vinegar powder

Heat the grapeseed oil in a tall-sided saucepan to 350°F. Gently fry the wonton skins until crisp and bubbled, jostling them around in the oil. Drain on paper towels and season aggressively with salt and malt vinegar powder.

CHILE OIL

MAKES 1 CUP

1 cup grapeseed oil
1 teaspoon Korean chile flakes

Warm the oil slightly and let the chile flakes bloom in the oil. Chill and keep in the refrigerator for up to a week.

PICKLED GOLDEN RAISINS

MAKES 2 CUPS

1½ cups golden raisins
1 cup cider vinegar
½ cup water
½ cup raw sugar
1 tablespoon Korean chile flakes
1 teaspoon fennel seeds, toasted
1 teaspoon kosher salt

Put the raisins in a heat-safe container. Bring all the other ingredients to a boil in a saucepan over high heat. Once boiling, remove from the heat and pour over the raisins. Let sit for at least an hour before using. The pickled raisins will keep for up to 2 months.

CASHEW CREAM

MAKES 2 CUPS

1½ cups raw cashews, soaked in water overnight
1 cup water
2 tablespoons fresh lemon juice
1 teaspoon kosher salt

Drain the soaked cashews and rinse with fresh water. Place the cashews in a high-powered blender. Add the water, lemon juice, and salt and blend, starting slowly and gradually increasing the speed. Blend on high until super smooth. You may have to add a little more water or agitate the cashews while blending on low to get the whole thing going. Check the seasoning for more salt if needed. It should have a consistency slightly looser than sour cream. You can omit the lemon juice if you want to use the cashew cream in place of heavy cream, such as in creamy soups.

HAMMERED MUSHROOMS

MAKES 2 CUPS

2 pounds button mushrooms, thinly sliced

2 tablespoons extra virgin olive oil

1½ tablespoons maple syrup

1 tablespoon Korean chile flakes

Preheat the oven to 375°F. Line two baking sheets with parchment paper.

Toss the sliced mushrooms with the olive oil, maple syrup, and chile flakes in a medium bowl until they are evenly coated. Season with salt and pepper. Divide the mushrooms evenly between the two pans and spread into a single layer. Bake for 25 minutes. Toss the mushrooms with a spoon and return to the oven. Continue to cook the mushrooms, checking on them every 10 minutes or so and stirring every time you check. The mushrooms are done when they are a deep brown color (but not burned) and slightly dried out—dried at the edges and firm in the center. Remove from the oven and let cool a little before using.

POLENTA PLANKS

MAKES ABOUT 12 PLANKS

Extra virgin olive oil

7 cups water

2 cups high-quality polenta (we use Anson Mills)

Kosher salt

Lightly grease a quarter sheet pan or an 8-inch square baking pan with a little bit of olive oil.

Bring the water to a boil in a medium saucepan over high heat. Add salt and taste the water—it should taste well seasoned. While whisking, pour the polenta into the boiling water. Simmer for 15 to 20 minutes, whisking occasionally. When ready, check the seasoning again for salt and then carefully pour the hot polenta into the pan and smooth the top as evenly as possible. Let set up at room temperature for at least 30 minutes. It will cut most easily into clean pieces if refrigerated for a couple hours or overnight. Cut into 12 planks.

CHEESY BRINED TOFU

MAKES 2 CUPS

1 pound extra firm tofu, drained well, coarsely crumbled or cut into 1½-inch cubes

½ cup white miso

½ cup nutritional yeast flakes

1½ tablespoons cane sugar

2 teaspoons kosher salt

¼ cup white wine vinegar

Place the tofu in a large, sealable, heat-safe container. In a medium saucepan, combine the miso, nutritional yeast, sugar, salt, white wine vinegar, and 4 cups water and place over medium-high heat. Bring to a boil, whisking often to completely dissolve the miso. Once the mixture is boiling, remove from the heat. Carefully pour the hot brine over the tofu. Let cool to room temperature before refrigerating. This should sit for at least 4 hours before it is used to allow the flavors to fully infiltrate the tofu. It will only get better when it is refrigerated overnight or even a couple of days.

PASTRAMI TOFU

**MAKES 1 BLOCK,
SERVES 6**

¾ cup black peppercorns

½ cup coriander
   seeds, toasted

¼ cup crushed red
   pepper flakes

½ teaspoon ground cinnamon

¼ cup kosher salt

3 garlic cloves, finely chopped

1 cup dry white wine

½ cup firmly packed dark
   brown sugar

1 pound extra firm
   tofu, drained, cut into
   ½-inch slabs

4 tablespoons grapeseed oil
   for searing

Maple syrup

Grind the peppercorns, coriander seeds, and red pepper flakes together in a spice grinder. Transfer to a medium bowl. Add the cinnamon, salt, garlic, white wine, and brown sugar to the bowl and mix to create a paste with the spices. Rub the outside of each tofu slab generously with about 2 tablespoons of the rub per slab. Place the slabs in a plastic storage container that has a tight-fitting lid—make sure to pack them in tightly. Sprinkle any remaining rub over the top of the tofu before sealing the container and putting it into the refrigerator. Let sit in the rub for about 4 days before using. When ready to use, rub off any excess seasoning from the outside of the slabs. Cut into ½-by-½-inch pieces. Sear in a hot pan with the grapeseed oil until they are golden brown and crispy. Right before they are finished, add a few tablespoons of maple syrup and let it caramelize and coat the exterior of the tofu. Serve hot.

CRUNCHY POTATOES

SERVES 6

2 pounds russet potatoes,
   peeled and cut into
   1½-inch pieces

Extra virgin olive oil

Place the cut potatoes in a large pot and fill with enough cold water to fully cover the potatoes. Season the water with plenty of salt. Bring up to a boil over high heat and reduce to a simmer. This is a good time to preheat the oven at 400°F. Cook the potatoes until it seems as though they are overcooked. They should be on the brink of falling apart and no longer have any sharp edges from being cut. Drain in a colander and return the potatoes to the now-empty pot. Add ¼ cup olive oil, along with salt and pepper, to the potatoes and stir gently to coat. Lightly grease two baking sheets with oil.

Divide the potatoes between the two baking sheets and spread into a single layer. Put into the oven and set a timer for 25 minutes. When the time is up, take the sheets out of the oven and use a metal spatula to scrape and flip the potatoes. The surface that was touching the sheets should be golden brown. Return the sheets to the oven and set a timer for another 15 minutes. When the time is up, flip the potatoes again. Keep cooking in 5-minute intervals until they are golden brown all over. Serve hot.

CONFIT POTATOES

SERVES 6

2 pounds small Yukon Gold or
   fingerling potatoes, sliced
   into ½-inch coins
4 cups grapeseed oil
2 tablespoons kosher salt
Spices, herbs, or aromatics

Place the sliced potatoes, grapeseed oil, salt, and flavorings in a large pot. Heat slowly over medium-low heat until bubbles just start to develop and rise to the surface from the potatoes. Reduce the heat to low and cook until the potatoes are tender, about 1 hour. Take the pot off the heat and let the potatoes sit in the oil for at least another hour. Using a strainer set over a large bowl, strain the potatoes, making sure to save the oil. The cooking oil can be refrigerated and reused up to three times.

MARINATED YUBA STRIPS

**MAKES 1 QUART
(ENOUGH FOR
2 POUNDS YUBA)**

¼ cup extra virgin olive oil
1 tablespoon freshly ground
   black pepper
1 tablespoon coriander
   seeds, toasted
1 cup roasted mushrooms

1 cup ground toasted walnuts
2 tablespoons ground coffee
   (Café Bustelo is our pick)
3 tablespoons dark
   brown sugar
1 tablespoon Dijon mustard
2 tablespoons nutritional
   yeast flakes
2 teaspoons Bragg
   Liquid Aminos
2 tablespoons malt vinegar
3 cups water or
   vegetable broth

2 pounds yuba, cut into
   ¼-inch strips

Combine the olive oil, pepper, coriander seeds, and roasted mushrooms in a medium saucepan over medium heat to toast the spices and release the smells.

Add all the other ingredients except the yuba and bring to a boil over medium-high heat. Reduce the heat and simmer for 15 minutes or so, until the sauce starts to thicken.

Meanwhile, unfold the yuba into a single sheet and cut it into ¼-inch strips that are about 3 inches long; put them into a large container. Once the sauce thickens, remove it from the heat. Carefully blend the sauce in small batches in a blender until smooth—add water if needed. Season with salt if needed. When the sauce is still hot, pour it over the yuba and let marinate for at least 1 hour.

BROWN RICE

MAKES 2 CUPS

1 cup high-quality brown rice
(we use Koda Farms)

1½ cups water

Kosher salt

Toast the rice in a medium pot over medium heat—no oil needed—stirring constantly until it begins to smell nutty. Add the water and a hefty pinch of salt to the pot and turn the heat up to high. Once the water has come to a rolling boil, reduce the heat to low, cover the pot with a sheet of aluminum foil with a few holes poked in it, and let cook for 35 to 40 minutes. Turn off the heat when the rice is just about done and let steam for another 15 minutes, covered, but off the heat. Either use right away or cool on a baking sheet, put into a sealed container, and refrigerate for up to 2 days until ready to use.

CORN BREAD

SERVES 9

2 cups soy milk

3 teaspoons white
wine vinegar

1½ cups corn flour

1 cup all-purpose flour

¼ cup medium-
grind cornmeal

6 tablespoons cane sugar

1 tablespoon baking powder

¾ teaspoon baking soda

1 teaspoon kosher salt

3 tablespoons grapeseed oil

¼ cup coconut oil (liquid)

Preheat the oven to 400°F. Grease a 9-inch square baking pan and line the bottom with parchment paper.

Whisk together the soy milk and white wine vinegar in a medium bowl and let sit. In a large bowl, combine the corn flour, all-purpose flour, cornmeal, sugar, baking powder, baking soda, and salt. Whisk the grapeseed oil into the soy milk mixture. Pour the soy milk mixture into the flour mixture and, using a spatula, fold gently to combine. When nearly fully combined, add the coconut oil and mix until just incorporated. Pour the batter into the pan and bake for about 20 minutes, until it is firm to the touch. Let cool for a little bit.

This recipe can be modified—add 2 teaspoons Korean chile flakes and ½ teaspoon black pepper for a spicy and savory version. Stale corn bread can be crumbled up and toasted in the oven set to 325°F for 15 minutes or so.

CHICKPEA MAYO

MAKES 2 CUPS

½ cup liquid from a
chickpea can

20 individual chickpeas

1½ tablespoons Dijon mustard

2 tablespoons cider vinegar

1 tablespoon cane sugar

2 teaspoons kosher salt

2½ cups grapeseed oil

Combine the chickpea liquid, chickpeas, mustard, cider vinegar, sugar, and salt in a tall container just large enough to fit the head of an immersion blender. Blend at high speed until the mixture is completely smooth and all the whole chickpeas are broken down. While the blender is running, slowly drizzle in the grapeseed oil. As you add the oil, an emulsion will form and it will begin to thicken. Check the seasoning for salt and sugar. This will keep, covered, in the refrigerator for about 1 week.

SPECIAL SAUCE

MAKES ABOUT 2 CUPS

1 cup Chickpea Mayo
  (page 211)

½ cup Roasted Red Tomatoes
  (page 71)

¼ cup ketchup

¼ cup hot chile sauce

1 tablespoon red wine vinegar

Combine all the ingredients in a tall container just large enough to fit the top of an immersion blender. Blend until smooth and the tomatoes are broken up. Season with salt, if necessary, and a little bit of pepper. This can also be done in a food processor.

SPICY MAYO

MAKES ABOUT 1 CUP

1 cup Chickpea Mayo
  (page 211)

3 tablespoons habanero
  hot sauce (we like
  Matouk's Calypso)

Mix together the mayo and hot sauce with a whisk. Hold, covered, for up to 3 days in the refrigerator.

SORRY, WE ARE
CLOSED

HOURS OF OPERATION:
MONDAY: 11:30AM-10PM
TUESDAY: CLOSED
WEDNESDAY: 11:30AM-10PM
THURSDAY: 11:30AM-10PM
FRIDAY: 11:30AM-10PM
SATURDAY: 11:30AM-10PM
SUNDAY: 11:30AM-10PM

THANK YOU.

ACKNOWLEDGMENTS

SUPERIORITY BURGER WOULD NOT HAVE BEEN POSSIBLE WITHOUT THE CONTRIBUTIONS, ASSISTANCE, ADVICE, AND GUIDANCE OF THE FOLLOWING PEOPLE:

Sunny Shokrae

Walter Green

Johan Kugelberg

Arlo Rosner

Dominic Masi

Dave Elliott

Claire Mysko

Lacey Romano

Ian Svenonius

Meredith Erickson

Rick Easton

Ashley Pulley

Ryan Healey

Charlotte Druckman

Lagusta Yearwood

Lizzi Bougatsos

Brian Degraw

Adam Nathanson

Sam McPheeters

Sheryl Rivas

Brett Lymon

Mac Mccaughan

Layla Gibbon

Lacey Burke

Sara Parenti

Agatha Kulaga

Kim Witherspoon

Jill Bialosky

Franca Tantillo

Edith Varela

Christina Brown

Bryan Novello

Tyler Jopek

Tim Midyett

Dave Rizo

Steve Albini

Gustavo Mendez

Darcy Spence

Fransico Garcia

Stephanie Sacchi

Jesse Pearson

Zachary Dillon

Atiba Jefferson

Jessica Koslow

Rick Bishop

Mariko Munro

Scotty Blenkarn

Brette Warshaw

Javier Villegas

Eliseo Hernandez

Francisco Morales

Javier Navas

Mateo Gonzalez

Maria Fabbrini

Mark Ladner

Jj Basil

Elisha Benhaim

Molly Mullholland Fitch

Steve Dore

Gavin Brown

Wendy Yao

Sheryl Heefner

Jr Reynolds

Millicent Souris

Jeff Kozlowski

Nelson Bermejo

Cruz Nieves

Chris Field

Jessi Okamoto

Kellie Quarton

Ryan Race

Dana Cree

Madeleine Perlmutter

Peter Meehan

GLOSSARY

BLACK-EYED PEAS Regular supermarket stuff is fine for soups where these beans play a supporting role. If you are serving them straight, say with just olive oil and salt, then search out a fancier brand like Rancho Gordo.

BRAGG LIQUID AMINOS Similar to soy sauce, and *senza glutine,* as the Italians would say. It's also total hippie natural food store stuff. Hard-griddled tofu deglazed with Bragg Liquid Aminos tastes eerily like grilled chicken.

BROCCOLI RABE A bitter green that bears almost no resemblance to actual broccoli. It has leaves and flowers and stalks that all taste slightly different, which is part of the fun. To put it in musical terms, rabe has a clean attack, and a satisfying decay.

CANE SUGAR, UNBLEACHED We use this as a 1:1 swap out for granulated white sugar. Sometimes (although not across the board) bone char is used in purifying and whitening sugar industrially. It's an old-fashioned practice that is getting phased out. Use cane sugar and you are in the clear, though.

CANNED TOMATOES We use high-quality imported Italian tomatoes almost exclusively. They just taste better. You can also score some cans from New Jersey, an underrated tomato-growing locale. Buy the whole ones and run them through a food mill to activate your inner *nonna.*

CHICKPEA CAN LIQUID Someone (no one knows exactly who) discovered a few years ago that the thick sludge usually discarded from a can of chickpeas can be useful for all sorts of things. You can add sugar and whip it into a stable meringue; you can use it as an egg substitute for leavening and emulsifying. We still do not totally understand how or why it works, but it thickens up our vegan mayo like a champ.

COCONUT MILK Look for real coconut milk, not coconut water, and not fake coconut milk that's just coconut extract and water thickened with xanthan gum.

COCONUT OIL We use it for vegan baking. It will impart a slight coconut flavor, but it's the closest thing to butter we have found, and it makes for a flaky and/or tender cookie or crust. It is solid when cold.

DEXTROSE We use this in our sorbet bases. It's a type of sugar that's less sweet than cane sugar, comes powdered, and aids with the creamy texture that is a hallmark of a finessed sorbet.

FAVA BEANS One of the most delicious, expensive, and pain-in-the-ass beans to deal with. They require multiple peeling sessions, but when they are at their spring peak, they are worth all the extra time and very low yield. For an off-season soup, find some decent frozen ones that are already peeled and ready to go, and you will be fine.

FENUGREEK A seed used a lot in Southeast Asian and Ethiopian cooking. Visually, it looks very similar to the boxed candy Nerds. It tastes slightly like maple syrup with a curried edge (which makes sense, considering its ubiquity in curry powders).

FRESH KELP Not the easiest thing to get your hands on, but when you can, then seize the opportunity. It's not gross, and it's doesn't taste like stuff to sprinkle in a fish tank. Fresh kelp has a clean oceanic flavor, is outrageously nutritious, has a textural bounty of chew, and is one of the most sustainable food sources around.

GOLDEN BALSAMIC VINEGAR Less cloying than cheap grocery store dark balsamic, less expensive than fancy balsamic, but still adds tartness and sweetness. We are particularly fond of deglazing a hot pan of fried tofu or vegetables with golden balsamic.

HALLOUMI Look for a vegetable rennet version, meaning it was coagulated without a cow's stomach lining, and is therefore vegetarian. It's a firm cheese that holds up well when fried or griddled. Brined tofu can replace this if you are looking for a vegan alternative.

KOHLRABI A biennial brassica that's related to cabbage and turnips and can be eaten cooked or raw. It's always at the greenmarket in NYC—full of leaves and stems (both very edible) in the summer, and crated up in rooty mounds in the winter.

KOREAN CHILE FLAKES A mild chile used traditionally in kimchi preparations. We use it when we want some fragrant heat, but don't want to go overboard with the spicing.

LABNE A strained kefir cheese very similar to Greek yogurt. If you are looking for a vegan alternative, there are a few ace coconut and cashew yogurts available at your local natural foods shop.

MALT VINEGAR Imparts a formidable boardwalk French fry flavor. It is not gluten-free though, so be sure to use it only when that isn't an issue.

MALT VINEGAR POWDER Available from a reputable spice purveyor. It adds a salt-and-vinegar potato chip quality, but no moisture.

NONMODIFIED POTATO STARCH We use this as a binder for the Superiority Burger. We initially used eggs, but a slurry of water and potato starch works splendidly and, let's face it, eggs are questionably vegetarian, right?

NUTRITIONAL YEAST Available in powder and flakes, imparts a cheesy flavor to things, it's totally vegan, and is also a good source of vitamin B_{12}, which is more commonly found only in mammal flesh.

OLIVE OIL The best sauce. Use it liberally. A blended cheaper oil is fine for frying and sautéing, and a more expensive specimen is to use as a finishing sauce.

PARSLEY We like both kinds (curly and Italian flat-leaf) for different applications. Parsley is funny; it seems like it's just hanging around not doing anything. But take it away and boy, do you miss it.

POLENTA We use Anson Mills Spin Rossa della Valsugana Polenta Integrale polenta exclusively. It is nothing like instant polenta, and doesn't take that much longer to cook. It has an irregular grain and cooks into a luscious corn pudding that can be served very soft or left to harden slightly so it can be sliced into wedges and browned in a hot pan.

POMEGRANATE MOLASSES A thick, sticky syrup that also has a pleasing tartness. Good when combined with opposing flavors. We griddle jalapeños and cover with pomegranate molasses, allowing the peppers to both thin the syrup, reduce the sweetness by releasing water, and add a bracing heat.

RAW CASHEWS Available at a reliable health food store or online. Make sure to stick your nose in the can or bag and really take a big whiff. If it smells off or sour, don't use the nuts. They should smell like nothing, in a good way.

SEASONED RICE WINE VINEGAR This is rice wine vinegar with sugar and salt already added. We refer to it as Superiority fish sauce even though it

tastes and acts nothing like fish sauce. A few drops in a salad or warm vegetable dish can zap the whole thing back to life.

SHISO Also known as perilla, this is one of our favorite herbs. It is used copiously in Japanese cuisine and has a flavor that straddles mint and basil while tasting wholly like itself. It adds a brightness in appropriately complementary flavor applications.

TAHINI Sesame paste. We use it a lot for sauces and even to coat and roast vegetables. A lot of tahini is rancid tasting. Look for slightly more expensive stuff. We use gallons and gallons of the Soom brand.

TAMARI Very similar to soy sauce, but often contains no wheat, therefore making it suitable for gluten-free preparations. We find the flavor to be deeper and richer than soy sauce. Also, tamari is total old-school health food store stuff so we are hooked.

TAMARIND Typically used in tropical climate (where it grows) cuisines as a sweetener. It is available frozen, dried, and in extract forms. All of these are pretty good, the extract being the least messy.

TOFU Soybean curd. The cheap stuff tastes weird. The pricier stuff tastes much better. A lot of people will tell you they hate tofu, which means they have probably been exposed to only the cheap stuff.

TOMATO PASTE We use the imported Italian stuff that comes in a toothpaste tube; it's more expensive than normal supermarket canned paste, and is worth every extra dollar. We usually fry it in olive oil until it morphs from bright red to a brownish brick red in order to caramelize the natural sugars and develop a lot of extra flavor.

TURBINADO SUGAR Coarse-grained organic sugar. Very texturally rewarding.

WONDRA FLOUR This is pre-gelatinized flour that has already been cooked so it doesn't need the long periods of cooking time required by raw flour. We use it to get very crisp French fried onions to top our Sloppy Dave sandwich.

YUBA The skin that forms on soymilk when it is gently heated, not unlike milk skin. Fresh, this is chewy and satisfying and can be flavored and griddled to taste like just about anything. It's also available dried, which more often than not tastes like chemicals.

INDEX

Note: Page numbers in *italics* refer to illustrations.